PLAYING THE GAME ONE PITCH AT A TIME

HEADS-UP
BASEBALL

KEN RAVIZZA
TOM HANSON

*Addval—
Have fun with the
Mental Game! Keep it
One Thing at a Time!
Breathe Deep
Ken Ravizza*

To Order This Book:
Kinesis: Heads Up Baseball
P. O. Box 7000-717
Redondo Beach, CA 90277
Send $17.95 + $1.25 Tax if CA Resident
Make Check Payable to **Kinesis**

Library of Congress Cataloging-in-Publication Data

Ravizza, Ken, 1948–
    Heads-up baseball : playing the game one pitch at a time /
by Ken Ravizza and Tom Hanson.
       p.   cm.
    ISBN 1-57028-021-5
    1. Baseball—Psychological aspects. 2. Motivation
(Psychology).   I. Hanson, Tom, 1962–   . II. Title.
GV867.6.H35   1994
796.357—dc20   94-47936
                                 CIP

Cover design by Peter Chu
Cover photograph: Manny Ramirez. Copyright © Jed Jacobson/Allsport
Edited by Kim Heusel
Text layout by Kim Heusel
Graphics by Suzanne Lincoln
Photographic reproduction assistance by Terry Varvel
Illustrations by Grant Emery Copeland
All interior major-league player photos by V. J. Lovero
All other inside photos by Katherine Mittnight unless otherwise credited

Published by Masters Press
A division of The McGraw-Hill Companies.
4255 West Touhy Avenue, Lincolnwood (Chicago), Illinois 60712-1975 U.S.A.
Copyright © 1995 by Ken Ravizza and Tom Hanson
All rights reserved. No part of this book may be reproduced, stored in a retrieval
system, or transmitted in any form or by any means, electronic, mechanical,
photocopying, recording, or otherwise, without the prior written permission of
the publisher.
Printed in the United States of America
International Standard Book Number: 1-57028-021-5
   13 14 15 16 17 18 19 RCP/RCP 0 9 8 7 6

Heads up out there!

"Heads-Up Baseball will teach you many things about the mental game, but for me, learning to have a routine that keeps me focused on things I have control of has been most helpful. It helps me sustain my focus in major-league baseball."
— **Tim Salmon, 1993 American League Rookie of the Year**

"This is a great book. It keeps things simple and does an excellent job of integrating the mental and physical aspects of the game. I ordered copies for my whole program."
— **Skip Bertman, head coach, LSU, national champions 1991 and 1993**

"Their ideas are just as important to softball as they are to baseball. Ken has worked with my team for the past 15 years, so I know the book is based on countless hours of watching and talking with coaches and athletes."
— **Judi Garman, softball coach, Cal State-Fullerton**

"As teachers and coaches, we constantly hear about the importance of the mental aspects of the game. This book provides practical, easy exercises that can be used to help you develop and refine your mental game. I use the information in this book all the time."
— **Rick Down, hitting coach, New York Yankees**

"When I'm recruiting, I look at a player's emotional maturity as much as his physical ability. I want a player to come in with a good head on his shoulders. At this level, games are won by the team that keeps its composure and intensity throughout the season. This book can help a player mature more rapidly."
— **Jerry Weinstein, pitching coach, U.S. Olympic Team**

"High school players should see this as required reading. Any coach who wants to take his team to a higher level of achievement should work this into his program."
— **Steve Gullotti, baseball coach, El Dorado High School**

"This book will help coaches work with their players on a more personal level. It's an important contribution to baseball."
— **John McNamara, former major-league manager**

Dedication

To Claire, my wife and best friend, for her support through all this; to Monica and Nina for their understanding; and to my parents for their love and for teaching me the meaning of the word "quality." — K.R.

To my parents for the love and opportunities they have given me. — T.H.

To the athletes and coaches who have shared their thoughts with us over the years. This book is the result of what we have learned from them. — K.R and T.H.

Acknowledgments

Special thanks to Jim Tehan for his listening and editorial support. We are particularly grateful for the wisdom shared by Marcel Lachemann, Joe Maddon and Dave Snow. Doug Newburg, Katherine Mittnight, Hank Aaron, Jim Abbott and V.J. Lovero were each critical to the success of this project as was the invaluable support from Skidmore College and the California State University at Fullerton. Kim Heusel's talented editing improved the book dramatically.

Thank you to the following people for their contributions: Jerry Weinstein, Rick Down, Wes Sime, Gary Mack, Ron Smith, Larry Corrigan, Bill Bavasi, Pat McMahon, Buck Rodgers, Sam Suplizio, Augie Garrido, Andrew Lorraine, Steve Rousey, Mike Weathers, Bert Blyleven, Bruce Hines, Don Sneddon, Skip Claprod, Norm Hayner, Rick Wolff, Neale Smith, Ken Forsch, Steve Gullotti, Denise Smith, Jeff Segrave, Phil Boshoff, John Danison, Ken Tangen, Jim Reese, Jerry Reuss, Mark Langston, Chuck Hernandez, Gene Mauch, Ken Hodge, Dave Winfield, Bob Boone, Bobby Grich, Kyle Abbott, Mike Gerakos, John McNamara, Bob Clear, Doug Rader, Ed Rodriquez, Howie Gershberg, Gary Ruby, Don Long, Tony Muser, Mike Couchee, Ray Lowenstein, Gary Stein, Chad Curtis, Mike Butcher, Kevin Flora, Dan Gould and, for being there, Chauncey Gardener.

We also are indebted to the California Angels, Long Beach State Dirtbags and Skidmore Thoroughbreds baseball teams for all they have taught us about the mental game.

Table of Contents

Preface

The cover of this book captures one of the great moments in baseball: the moment just before the pitch. The mental game that is played between pitches usually determines what happens on each pitch. Players and coaches often talk about the importance of playing "heads-up" baseball — anticipating the next play, being confident of success, totally focusing on each pitch — but few know how to learn or teach the mental aspects of the game. As a result, most of their attention is placed on the mechanical and technical aspects of the game, leaving the mental game to chance. Their old cliche "Either you've got it or you ain't" is an unnecessary approach.

This book provides you with an understanding of how the mental game works and details the concrete strategies for developing such elusive skills as concentration, mental preparation and staying in control under pressure. Most importantly, it gives you ways to help you take control of your confidence. This book is for the **player** interested in reaching his full potential. Although many of the concepts can be used by players of any age, the primary target group is high school level and beyond. Many exercises and worksheets are presented throughout the book. Doing these exercises and working on the techniques in practice is the only way you'll improve your mental game. Review the book regularly to develop and refine your mental skills as you progress through your season and career. Keep a pen handy — this should be a book you do, not just read. Like anything else, you'll get out of it what you put into it.

Working on the mental game is not a substitute for hard physical work. Regardless of how good your mental game is, if you are not putting in the effort on your physical body — getting strong and flexible, developing solid techniques in the various skills, and learning the strategies of the game — you will not find out how good you can be.

Although written primarily for players, **coaches** will find the book provides techniques they can use to help their players learn the mental side of the game. Our goals are to provide a language players and coaches can use for talking about the mental game, and generate concrete strategies to develop the heads-up style of play necessary to succeed in baseball. In addition to teaching their players these concepts, coaches will find the worksheets and exercises in the book to be valuable resources at practices and team meetings and as a basis for discussions on the mental game.

Although the examples in this book refer to baseball, **softball players** will find many of the concepts to be helpful. Only a minimal effort will help them improve their mental games.

Parents of ballplayers may find the book helpful in gaining additional insight into what it takes to play good baseball. Reading the book will enable them to direct their discussions with their child to positive, helpful topics, rather than simply focusing on the outcome of a game or at bat.

Finally, **fans** can enhance their enjoyment of the game when they fully understand what needs to be done to play well. For example, watching to see which players look like they're in control of themselves and playing the game one pitch at a time adds an extra dimension to the game.

Keep in mind that while you may see immediate improvement in your performance as a result of using the ideas in this book, this book is not a superficial, "quick-fix" scheme. Developing a strong mental game takes a sustained and dedicated effort throughout the season. If you want to be confident and focused when your team needs you to come through in the bottom of the last inning, you need to work on it in practice just as you would any physical or technical aspect of the game.

Similarly, this is not a "cookbook" prescribing THE right way to play baseball. Just as there are fundamentals to hitting that everyone needs to follow, but unlimited ways to execute them, there are many ways to execute the fundamentals of the mental game. Adopt the ideas that you like to your personal style in a way comfortable for you. We will constantly remind you to not let this get complicated; keep the game as simple as possible.

> One of the things we've done to help you keep things simple is to put boxes around the paragraphs containing the most important information. For a short and to-the-point version of the book, read the text in the boxes and the captions under the photos and drawings. When you're ready for the full story, read the entire text.

Finally, the principles found in this book can enhance your skills in the human race, not just the game of baseball. As you read, think of ways these ideas can improve your performance in all areas of your life.

Foreword

Baseball is one of the most difficult games in the world. It's always different; there's something new thrown at you every day. But adversity is part of what makes baseball such a great game, and I'm proud to say that I feel I faced — and overcame — about as much adversity as anybody. It's something you have to be able to overcome if you want to be the best player you can be.

For me, my ability to fully focus on what I had to do on a daily basis made me the successful player that I was. Sure, I had some natural ability, but that only gets you so far. I think I learned how to focus, it wasn't something I was necessarily born with. I realized early on that if I was going to reach my goal of being one of the best players ever to play the game, I had to do things other players weren't doing. I had to get my thoughts together. I've seen players with as much or more ability as I had but somewhere along the line they lost sight of what they were doing; they just couldn't keep in tune.

I could have been like that. I could have ended up with a .220 batting average, hitting 225 home runs and driving in 700 runs, but I wasn't going to be satisfied with that. I felt that if I wanted to be as good as my ability would allow, I had to do a lot of work on my own. A lot of that was on my mental game.

Most players don't understand what makes them good. For example, what makes you have a good day at the plate? It wasn't just that you hit some hanging curveball or that the pitcher made a mistake, it was because you were totally in control of what was happening. You saw the ball, your mind saw it, you had concentration and everything worked just right. But tomorrow is different, and what makes it different is your concentration. If you don't hit well tomorrow, it probably will be because you fail to focus.

Having great concentration and being in control of yourself are not things you decide to do one day, they're skills you have to develop over time. It's kind of like learning your ABC's as a child; you learn through repetition. It's not going to come to you overnight.

This book gets at the heart of what I feel is the most important part of the game. It can help you develop your ability to prepare yourself before you perform and concentrate while you perform. People always ask me about mechanics — where I put my hands, what I did with my wrists, and so on — but that's not it. I've never heard anyone talk about hitting the way the authors of this book talk about it. No matter what level you're on, to have the type of career you can be proud of, you have to take charge of your mental game. It's what can set you apart from other players.

Hank Aaron
All-time major-league leader
in home runs, extra-base hits,
total bases, runs batted in

Introduction

Wouldn't it be satisfying to look in the mirror at the end of your baseball career and say, "I gave the game all I had?" You pushed yourself to the peak of your potential, and the world saw the very best you had to offer.

Knowing no stone was left unturned and confident that you consistently performed at the top levels of your God-given abilities throughout your career would bring immense satisfaction. This perspective is why combining the mental side of baseball with its physical demands is so important. It's why this book is important. The questions and "what ifs" are eliminated.

Mastering the mental game is not easy. Most players spend 95-100 percent of their practice time focusing on the physical aspects of the game. As a result, physical adjustments are made from game to game, but some of the same mistakes occur no mat-

Jim Abbott

ter how hard we apply ourselves. Slowing it all down and analyzing our mental approach is a surprisingly effective way of becoming better baseball players. I know it's certainly helped me. I also know it's not easy, but neither is taking 50 extra swings in the batting cage or fielding 100 more grounders!

Players at every level struggle with the mental game, not allowing themselves to reach their potential. In the major leagues, it's said that a pitcher's control problems are 90 percent mental. A pitcher who has reached the major-league level can throw strikes, so if you are not throwing the ball over the plate something else is inhibiting you. That is where mental skills enter the fray. The player who overcomes these lapses wins — period.

Confidence is the most important part of pitching. It's a trust and inner belief in yourself. It's those feelings you have when everything goes right: the control is there, your pitches have life and movement, and nothing can shake you. Those moments are truly awesome.

But it's not like that every time out. There are nights when nothing comes easily, and those are the times when winning pitchers dig deep to summon that trust and confidently attack the hitter in crucial situations. It's easier for some than others to call upon their reserves of confidence (or even cockiness), but everyone can learn to draw up the confidence needed to win. When the pressure is on and the cleanup hitter is up with two outs in the eighth, we can develop the ability to draw a deep breath, stick out our chests, throw back our shoulders and say, "Here's my pitch, try to hit it!" It's an exhilarating feeling!

A slump is something every baseball player dreads, an endless period of time where nothing comes easily. Everyone offers advice, but nothing seems to help. A strong foundation in mental training is a big boost during these times, and this foundation is an indescribably valuable tool over the marathon of a season. Strong mental skills can prevent long slumps from happening at all, but if they do, setting attainable goals, having daily routines and developing consistent preparation skills build the confidence that finally gets you over the hump. The small successes resulting from your routines and preparation lead to positive feelings at game time.

Nervousness before games can be frightening. Developing relaxation and visualization strategies reduce this anxiousness. Setting aside some time to calm down and visualize a game plan hours before the game can make that first pitch much less imposing. After all, that's the only pitch you can do anything about right now anyway. Visualization brings a sense of confidence that you've been through this already and know exactly what it's going to take to do the job.

Baseball should be fun, but don't forget that it's also a tough sport. Even if you pay attention to every phase of your game, there is no guarantee of success in a traditional sense. The way you evaluate your performances can be altered by pressures from fans, statistics, the media and coaches, and they can be cruel in their conclusions. The degree of talent around you may seem so overwhelming that you wonder how you reached this point in the first place. But beneath it all, it's nice to know that those of us to whom the game doesn't come so easily can level the playing field.

Solid training in the mental game allows us to meet these obstacles head-on and play with every ounce of our ability. Rising to the challenges of great competition, we can then scrutinize our efforts by our own standards, and this is where a deeper enjoyment of the game occurs. This is what we strive for.

Bring on the game!

Jim Abbott
major-league pitcher

Fundamentals of Heads-Up Baseball

- Take responsibility for your thoughts and actions.

- Commit to a mission: know why you play baseball, what character traits you want to possess and what you want to accomplish in the game.

- Make your daily actions consistent with your mission.

- Play one pitch at a time, confident and focused on each pitch as it is played with disregard for past or future pitches.

- Focus on the process of playing the game rather than the outcomes of your performances.

- Realize that you can't control what happens around you, but you can control your response to it, and that you must be in control of yourself before you can control your performance.

- Develop your mental skills so you consistently perform near the best of your ability and have "something to go to" when faced with adversity.

- Practice what you are going to do in a game.

- Learn each day.

- Keep it simple.

Playing with Confidence

Scenario 1

Steve Jones is on the mound, but just barely. After four good innings, he opens the fifth by walking the leadoff batter then gives up hits to the next two. After the fourth batter is safe on an error, Steve gives up another walk and has just delivered ball one to the current hitter.

Steve is in a hurry to throw the next pitch. "Let's get out of this right now," he says to himself as everything seems to speed up around him. He's annoyed that his catcher is holding on to the ball, telling him to calm down. "I'm OK, damn it," he snaps back. His eyes shift from one place to another, not clearly focusing on anything. He notices a lot of hurried activity down in his team's bullpen and hears a sarcastic voice in the opposing dugout yell, "Throw it harder!"

Steve pulls on his jersey as if it is starting to squeeze him. It's almost time to stick a fork in Steve — he's about done.

Scenario 2

Frank Simmons is on fire. He's been hitting everything hard for the last couple of games. He looks totally relaxed at the plate: calm and focused. "I'm seeing the ball real well right now," he tells his teammates, who know that's probably the understatement of the year. The ball looks both big and slow to Frank which gives him plenty of time to decide on each pitch; there's no way anyone can throw the ball past him.

Although he studies the pitcher and each situation carefully, his mind is clear in the batter's box. He's not thinking; he's just an unstoppable hitting machine, oblivious to everything around him. He simply sees the ball and hits it. Frank can't wait for his next at bat because hitting is easy, his swing effortless. In short, Frank is in the "zone."

Do these scenarios sound familiar? This book will help you spend more time experiencing what Frank is experiencing. The goal of the mental game is to play with confidence. The goal of the mental game is to play with a sense of freedom, a sense of total concentration, high physical energy and a lack of fear. It's about trusting your ability and letting go.

More important, though, this book also explains the skills needed to handle situations like Steve, the pitcher, is facing — those all-too-frequent times when you lose confidence and feel yourself losing control.

Baseball is a mentally difficult game because every player must endure so much adversity and failure. Hitters who fail "only" 70 percent of the time are all-stars, and pitchers must endure the personal pressure of winning and losing games. Slumps, razzing from fans and opponents, injuries, poor umpiring, the slow pace of the game, long hours at the ballpark, poor field conditions, bad weather, and playing games on consecutive days add to the difficulty that no player escapes. It's pretty safe to say that if you aren't facing some adversity right now, it's on its way!

Players often allow negative events from one pitch to carry over into the next pitch causing them to "spiral out of control" and leaving them the difficult challenge of playing more than one pitch at a time.

We often see players spiral out of control. It can start with something relatively minor: a "bad" call by an umpire, walking a batter, misplaying a ball in the field, or swinging and missing at a pitch in the dirt. From there, you spiral out of control. You're upset about what happened on the previous pitch, fail to refocus, and screw up on the next pitch. Upset about the last two pitches (or perhaps the last two at bats), you screw up on the next one. Instead of a centered and balanced mind-set that leads to good performances, you snowball out of control. Instead of being focused on the present and playing one pitch at a time, you are, in effect, mentally **playing at least three pitches at a time!**

As you'll see, self-control is a major theme through **must be in control of yourself before you can control y**

Players generally agree that the game seems almost easy what is often called the "zone" roughly 10 percent of the ti question, then, is, "What do you do the other 90 percent of critical that you have something to go to when the game isn't and your confidence begins to slip. **Peak performance isn't about being perfect, it's about compensating and adjusting.**

> The players who get the most out of their ability recognize the mental game's importance and find ways to improve their mental skills. Part of what makes those players successful is their ability to adjust. They are consistently at or near their best even when they don't feel their best. Unfortunately, most players leave the mental game to chance, not realizing that a strong mental game can be developed.

Confidence: The Goal of the Mental Game

Clearly, confidence is the name of the game. Both professional and college players say that 80-100 percent of their performance on a given day is determined by their belief in their ability to succeed.

> *"Confidence is everything."*
> *— The opinion of just about every pro and college player you ask*

Confidence is described as a feeling, a belief or a knowing that the task at hand can be successfully performed. Whether that's getting a batter out, hitting the ball, making a defensive play, or stealing a base, the player has a sense of certainty that he'll get the job done. (For example, it's pretty safe to say that our man Frank is feeling confident at the plate right now.)

A confident player has strong positive thoughts and images running through his head. When he's thinking about baseball, he sees himself playing well and making great plays. He might not even be aware that he's "talking" to himself in a positive way. "I'm going to rip this guy," "He can't hit me," "Nothing can get by me," are common phrases that might be echoing through the confident player's mind.

Finally, you can observe the best players by the way they move, the presence they have. They look calm and in control. They don't use rushed or awkward gestures — they exude confidence. They stand tall, have their chests out and may even cross the line into what many would call cocky.

This combination of positive factors results in players feeling confident and looking forward to their next performance. Pitchers look forward to their next start, hitters are dying to get back up to the plate and fielders hope the next ball is hit to them.

Dave Winfield is well-known for his confident physical presence.

When you play with confidence you are playing "free" — free of fear, tension, worry, doubt and stress. These negative emotions — all of which are the results of your own thinking — are obstacles you put in your way. They are like mental speed bumps that slow the progress toward your goals.

As pictured in the diagram below, the goal is to play with confidence, to get to the point where you totally trust your skills and let yourself perform. Sometimes — roughly 10 percent of the time — you go straight there and "just do it."

The reality, though, is that most of the time you need to take the more difficult route, the route through mental skills.

MENTAL SKILLS

90%

CONFIDENCE

10%

YOU

The best players in the game play well even when they aren't feeling their best. With the information in this book, you can, too. We'll teach you mental skills in the same way you learn physical skills. After a basic idea is presented, a way to practice that skill is given. Like physical skills, mental skills don't develop overnight. Further, having solid mental skills won't guarantee success. What it will do is give you your best chance to be successful.

There is no substitute for hard, physical work. You have to "put the hay in the barn" to find out how good you can be. This book isn't a quick fix for your performance problems; rather, it presents concrete strategies based on time-tested principles of baseball performance that, if practiced consistently, will enhance your baseball abilities.

Taking Responsibility for Your Mental Game

Baseball centers around home plate. Other parts of the field are important, of course, but home is the hub around which everything else revolves. In the mental game, everything revolves around taking responsibility for your own thinking and performance.

As we mentioned, most athletes leave their thinking to chance. If they are playing well they are thinking confident thoughts and doing the things they need to do to play well. But if they are not playing well, their minds are filled with negative thoughts and they act as if the world was coming to an end. This, of course, leads to continued poor play!

Think about this: if you are 0-for-10 at the plate, why do you feel depressed or angry? If you've lost your last three pitching decisions do you have to lose your confidence?

Although these negative emotions may seem natural when things aren't going well, nothing forces you to feel this way. We mentioned earlier that fear, worry, tension, doubt, and other negative emotions are obstacles that get in the way of your performance. You have to realize that each of these is the result of **your own thinking**.

Look at it this way: none of these obstacles is found in the *Official Baseball Rulebook*. Nowhere does it say, "If the pitcher has walked the bases loaded, he shall put himself in a tense and angered state." Nor will you find, "If a batter has not hit safely in his last seven turns at bat, he must spend his time questioning whether he will ever get another hit."

Your mind means well; it wants to help, but it often gets in the way and keeps your body from performing at its peak — especially if your mind is unskilled.

The purpose of practicing your mental skills is to remove the obstacles you put in your way — obstacles that keep you from being confident. Taking responsibility for your thinking means choosing what to think and how to act rather than blindly reacting to events around you. You don't have to think any

> *"The price of greatness is responsibility."*
> — **Winston Churchill**

particular way or react to a situation with any particular emotion. Choose what you think about. Since your thoughts greatly influence how well you play — thinking confidently leads to playing well and thinking negatively leads to playing poorly — it's critical to choose your thoughts wisely. We emphasize throughout the book that **you can't control what happens to you, but you can control your reaction to it.**

Thus, the central idea is that you must take responsibility for your mental game. Your coach or your teammates can support you, but nobody can do it for you. The thoughts in your head largely determine how well you are going to play, and you are responsible for what goes on in your head.

Here is a brief summary of each player's mental game responsibilities.

Your Responsibilities Include:

1) **Having a clearly defined "mission."** Your mission clarifies why you play baseball, what type of player you want to be and what you want to accomplish in the game.

Your mission provides direction, intensity and purpose to your practice sessions and games. It also helps you deal with the day-to-day adversities that come with being a baseball player. If you are going to find out how good a player you can be, you've got to have some sense of being "on a mission." For example, what would you like your reputation to be as a ballplayer? Similarly, how would you like to be remembered as a ballplayer after you've hung up your spikes?

2) **Playing the game one pitch at a time.** Everyone plays the game one pitch at a time physically, but very few consistently play the mental game one pitch at a time. In essence, playing one pitch at a time means being as confident and as focused as possible on each pitch as it is thrown.

We break playing one pitch at a time into three basic steps:

Step 1: Be in Control of Yourself

The first step is getting yourself under control. To be in control of yourself you need to first be aware of what is going on inside you. Are you nervous or tight? Is your mind racing like our pitcher Steve's? Or are you confident, composed and relaxed like Frank? If you determine you're not in control of yourself, are you able to make the adjustments necessary to get where you want to be? In short, you must be able to recognize whether or not you are in control of yourself and then have the mental skills to make any necessary adjustments.

Step 2: Have a Plan or Purpose on Each Pitch

Once you are in control of yourself, clarify exactly what you want to accomplish on this next pitch. As a pitcher, decide what pitch to throw and where to throw it. As a hitter, know what you're trying to do at the plate. As a fielder, know what to do if the ball is hit to you.

Just as important as having a purpose on each pitch is making a commitment to your plan. For example: pitchers, how many times have you started out throwing a curveball and wondered half way through your windup if you should be throwing a fastball instead? Did you get that ball back or was it hit out of the yard? You've got to be committed to your plan.

Step 3: Trust Yourself

The final step to playing one pitch at a time is to trust yourself — to let yourself perform. You're under control, you know what you want to do, now just do it. This is the "free" feeling we discussed earlier. When you are playing with confidence, you are trusting yourself and letting go of conscious effort. You are not trusting yourself when you are trying hard, aiming the ball, muscling up or pressing.

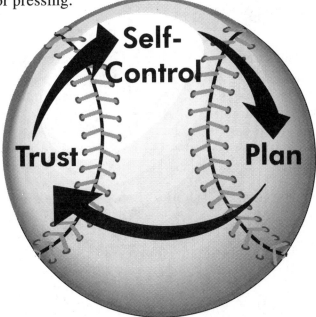

Coaches and players are aware that the game must be played "one pitch at a time" but nobody talks about **how to do it.** These three steps — self-control, having a plan, and trusting yourself provide concrete strategies for playing the game one pitch at a time.

3) Focus on the process rather than the outcome. This third responsibility is a tough one. Baseball is so oriented toward outcome statistics that players have difficulty evaluating themselves on how well they "worked the process" by using their pre-performance routines. Don't get us wrong, results such as batting average, RBIs, earned run average, and wins and losses are important. But to get the outcome you want, you must focus on the process of playing the game. This book promotes the idea that since the outcome of what you are trying to do (such as get a base hit or get a batter out) is outside of your control, you must focus your energies on the process of playing the game rather than on the results of your efforts.

> *"Results thinking is just a big trap. You've got to work on your physical and mental skills and then go out, trust what you've worked on and accept the results."*
> **— Dave Snow, Long Beach State head baseball coach**

4) Develop your mental skills. Just as you need to develop physical skills such as throwing off-speed pitches, hitting to the opposite field and fielding balls to your backhand side, you need to develop some key mental skills if you are going to discover just how good a ballplayer you can be. These skills include the deep breath, mental imagery, self-talk, preperformance routines

Hank Aaron, seen here hitting his 710th home run, said his ability to focus was something he learned to do. (National Baseball Library, Cooperstown, N.Y.)

and daily goal setting. These skills become your "something-to-go-to" when the pressure is on. They give you the ability to make the adjustments that are so critical to success in baseball.

5) Make a commitment to learning. The reason baseball has such an extensive minor-league system is that there is so much to learn about the game before it can be played at its highest level. You are already showing an interest in learning by the fact that you're reading this book. Way to go. Making a commitment to learning as much as you can each day is a vital part of finding out how good you can be. One of your main perspectives on the game should be to learn as much as possible, but we'll emphasize two points in particular.

First, it's important that you get into the habit of constructively evaluating each of your performances. Mentally replaying your at bats after a game, for example, can turn four at bats into eight or 12, helping make you a more "experienced" player. Even a bad performance such as making two errors or giving up a game-winning home run can be turned into a positive experience if you take a little time and draw a lesson or two from it.

Second, we'll stress the importance of quality practice sessions. Practices are really where the action is. You can't expect a skill to simply show up in a game if you haven't practiced it first. You might think that the biggest thing your mental game needs help with is keeping your composure in the last inning of a one-run ball game, but the real focus should be on the quality of your practices. If you do the work on your mental game in practice, you will be able to handle pressure situations in games.

These are what we feel your responsibilities are in the mental game. Your coach can help you with each of these things, but nobody can do them for you: they are your responsibility.

Exercise: **Understanding Your Ups and Downs**

An important idea that runs throughout this book is that we want you to become more aware of the relationship between what you think about and how well you play.

Since your primary goal is to get totally confident and trust yourself, you first need to get clear on what goes on for you when you are trusting yourself, when you are in the "zone." It also is helpful to examine the thinking that contributed to your worst performances. If you do a good job answering the questions on the following page, you'll have a clear target for your mental game as well as an improved understanding of how your thoughts impact your performance. You may want to write your answers to these and other questions throughout the book in a journal. Recording your thoughts each day is an invaluable aid to your performance.

Write your response to each question as it relates to your **BEST** performance in baseball in the column on the left and your response as it relates to your **WORST** performance in the column on the right.

	<u>Best</u>	<u>Worst</u>
Who were you playing against?		
What were your thoughts before the game?		
What were you thinking or saying to yourself at the time of your performance?		
How would you describe your emotional state at the time?		
What was your focus during your performance?		
What, if anything, was different about the way you experienced your performance (i.e., Was the ball bigger? Did the action seem faster or slower than usual?, etc.)		

Compare your two sets of responses. What are the differences in your mental approach to your best and worst performances?

The Coach's Box

What thoughts and actions lead to your best coaching performances? What is your focus before and during your best practices?

Coaching is performing, so think of how you can apply each idea and exercise in this book to yourself. These skills will make you a more effective coach and a more credible teacher of heads-up baseball. You need to be a role model of the confidence and self-control you want your players to possess on the field. Your players are more likely to be confident if they sense you are!

As you interact with your players, keep in mind that confidence is the most important element in the game. Get into the habit of asking yourself, "How can I help this player or team be more confident?"and, "How will what I'm doing or saying affect this guy's belief in himself?"

Caution

As you begin to work with the ideas on the following pages, don't lose sight of the fact that they are there to help you focus your intensity and emotions, not take them away. Players new to this material sometimes get so involved with the mental game that they forget to go out and compete. Work the process with the will to win.

2

Going on a Mission

Pretend for a moment that you're attending an end-of-the-season banquet in honor of **your retirement from baseball.** You may be retiring from any level of baseball — high school, college, professional or an amateur league, but after all these years you've decided to hang it up. All of your friends, relatives, former teammates and coaches are there. After a pleasant meal (probably grilled chicken), a coach or player you have chosen talks about you and your baseball career. After a few humorous put-downs and highlights of your accomplishments in the game, he speaks on your character — on how you played the game.

What would he say? What would you want him to say?

When athletes talk about a successful season, they often use the phrase, "We were on a mission." "We pulled together," they continue, "because we were all after the same thing." A player talking about a game in which he played well often feels this way. "I knew exactly what I wanted to do and I just went out and did it," he might say.

You probably know individuals who come up short because they didn't have a mission. "The guy has all the tools in the world but he doesn't do anything with them," is a typical statement. "He's got no sense of direction. If somebody would light a spark under him he'd be a great player." A team that lacks a sense of mission often fails to perform up to its capabilities. The theme of this chapter is motivation, which is pretty much the theme for everything in baseball. Nothing happens without it.

Our task isn't to motivate you — only you can do that. That may be a cliche, but it's true. No big emotional speech is going to carry you through the day-to-day blood, sweat and tears needed to succeed in baseball. To be the best you can be, the fire must come from within. You are responsible for your own motivation.

This chapter helps you clarify why you play baseball, what type of player you want to be and what you want to accomplish in the game. Understanding the role of a mission and getting yours clarified can heighten your intensity, sharpen your focus and toughen your mental skills. No player will be as good as he can be without a strong sense of being "on a mission."

What Is a Mission and Why Is It Important?

Your answers to three questions can put your mission in focus:

1) Why do you play baseball?

2) What type of player would you like to be?

3) What would you like to accomplish in baseball?

The first question examines your motivation for playing baseball. Players often say they "love the game" or "enjoy the competition."

The second question focuses on the character traits you want to possess, or what you would like your reputation as a ballplayer to be. Responses might include "plays with intensity," "is a consistent player," or "gets the most from his ability."

The third question refers more to tangible outcomes such as winning a championship, hitting .300 or playing in the major leagues.

How would you answer these questions? Take a minute to think about your answers and keep them in mind as we explain the importance of a clearly defined mission.

MINIMIZES STRESS   DIRECTION   INTENSITY

MISSION

MEANING   DISCIPLINE

1) Your Mission Gives Direction and Defines Discipline

Knowing your mission and keeping it prominent in your mind gives direction to your actions. Most players let their physical feelings dictate how well they play. If they feel good they think they'll play well; when they don't feel good, their performance usually suffers.

Heads-up players, however, are driven by values, a sense of purpose and their mission. Baseball can be a grind and at times you may not feel like making the effort that will take you closer to your dream. It takes discipline and commitment to work hard every day. If part of your mission is to play hard every day, you have to play hard today!

> Discipline and commitment are defined as putting your mission first. You do what your mission "says" you should do rather than what you feel like doing. Committed athletes are driven by their purpose and not by how they happen to feel on a given day.

Clarifying your mission gives you something to go to when you don't feel like doing what you need to do or some adversity gets in your way. It provides you with a ready-made, honest answer to the question, "Why am I doing this?" when you are in the outfield running sprint after sprint, rehabilitating an injured shoulder in the training room, fielding ground balls on an infield full of bad hops, turning down an invitation to go out on the town, or any other time you might not feel like doing what you are doing.

Attitude Is A Decision

Making decisions is easier for players who have a mission because their priorities are set. When a mission is clear the question is, "When am I going to work out today?" not, "Should I work out today?" There's a big difference between these attitudes.

2) Your Mission Provides Meaning

Clarifying your mission keeps you focused on the reason you play baseball and the meaning it has for you.

What is the meaning of baseball? It may seem irrelevant at first, but all we're really asking is, "What do you get out of playing baseball?" If there is no purpose in playing you wouldn't do it.

Trying to find meaning in baseball brings to mind the Greek story of Sisyphus. A long time ago, Sisyphus eavesdropped on a conversation the gods were having about the meaning of life. Mortals weren't supposed to hear what the gods talked about in their private meetings, and they were upset when Sisyphus came back and told his friends what the meaning of life was.

Sisyphus was tried and found guilty. As was the custom, Sisyphus' sentence was very creative. The gods decided Sisyphus would push a large rock up a long, steep hill until he reached the top. Then the rock would roll to the bottom of the hill and Sisyphus would have to start all over again. This he would do for eternity.

The gods were quite pleased with the punishment and sat back to watch Sisyphus go at it. They watched Sisyphus take a different approach each time he pushed the rock up the hill. The first time he got a feel for what the rock and hill were like. The next time he went as fast as he could, the third time he tried to see how gracefully he could push the rock, and the fourth time he tried to see how slowly he could push it. Each time he had a different purpose in mind.

Because he had a **purpose**, Sisyphus stayed **focused** on his task and pushed the rock with intensity. He actually enjoyed the challenge of coming up with different ways to push the rock and took pride in that ability. In all, he did a great job of pushing that rock.

Playing baseball is a lot like Sisyphus' task. Each day the field is prepared, you warm up and the game begins with the same rules and the same score, 0-0. Once you play that game, regardless of what happened, that big rock rolls down the hill and you start again the next day.

> What is the meaning of baseball? The meaning comes from you. You decide what to put into it and what you get out of it. You have to push a lot of rock to play the game well, so work to develop some sense that what you are doing makes a difference to you. The more meaning you bring to playing baseball, the more you get out of it.

3) Your Mission Minimizes Stress

You always hear people say, "You've got to keep it in perspective," but what does that mean? It means seeing the big picture and understanding how baseball fits into life. Knowing why you play baseball and what you want to get out of it gives you perspective.

Many players tie their feelings of self-worth to their performance. It's easy to fall into this trap when a lot of your time is spent thinking about baseball and much of the attention you receive from other people is related to baseball. When friends ask, "How's baseball going?" you naturally see it as an indication that that's what you're all about. When you think your value as a person is on the line each time you go up to bat, you're going to be nervous. With so much on the line, how could you not feel pressured?

But if you decide that you play baseball because you love it and that you are OK regardless of how you perform, you are less likely to feel stress during a game. If you love it, why get so upset? The less stress you experience, the better you play! The better you understand the big picture, the more likely you are to free yourself up and play great.

4) Your Mission Fuels Intensity

Having a clear sense of being "on a mission" adds "intensity" to your game. When present moment to present moment you have an intent, it results in your having intensity. That's where the word intensity comes from. You need to have something to focus on and strive for or you will end up going through the motions. Taking 15 ground balls with game-like intensity is more valuable than taking 100 when you're just going through the motions. When you have a purpose in mind, you add quality to your performance.

A clear sense of your mission gives a sense of direction, discipline and meaning. It also helps minimize the stress and fuels intensity. In short, it helps you play heads-up baseball.

Now let's move on to the task of clarifying your mission.

Why Do You Play Baseball?

This is a simple but powerful question. Many players experience problems with the mental aspects of the game when they lose sight of the reasons they play the game.

Why do **you** play baseball? Write your answer(s) below.

_____

_____

_____

_____

_____

The most common responses include, "I love the game," the competition," "it's fun," "the relationships with my teammates," and "the difficulty of the game."

Baseball is a difficult game, so if you love playing it, you must, in some way, love the difficulties it presents. If you enjoy the competition, you must at some (well-hidden) level enjoy the "failure" that comes with it. Would you honestly love it if you succeeded all of the time? (If you just want to win, go play eight- and nine-year-olds every day.)

If you play because you enjoy the relationships with your teammates, don't let a slump stop you from having a good time with your buddies. Having a few laughs in the dugout can loosen you up when you're on the field and enable you to play better.

Keeping the reason you play baseball prominent in your mind will enhance your enjoyment of the game and help you avoid the fear, tension and doubt that so often get in the way of your performance.

What Type of Player Do You Want to Be?

This is an important question because your answer serves all the purposes we discussed above and is totally within your control. You can choose to play with pride and see how much you can learn each day. You can't choose to be the winning pitcher in today's game because too many things are outside of your control. Remember, spend your time and energy on the things you can control.

To help you in your thinking about this question, here's how some successful players have answered it.

Don Mattingly   **Tony Gwynn**

Their approaches to baseball have made them two of the most respected players in the game.

Characteristics of Successful Players

Think of a major-league player you admire. What is it, in addition to his natural ability, you admire? Maybe you thought of Roger Clemens' work ethic, Ozzie Smith's consistency and durability, Tony Gwynn's commitment to excellence or Chuck Knoblauch's hard-nosed attitude. The traits you admire in others say a lot about the type of player you'd like to be and may make up the foundation of your mission in baseball.

Great players have many different traits; no single trait must be held by every player to be successful. But after studying and interacting with great players, a few traits emerge that nearly all seem to possess.

Below is a partial list of characteristics that champion athletes in all sports tend to have:

courage	honesty	dedication	sportsmanship
fun	unselfishness	enjoyment	mental toughness
focus	leadership	composure	concentration
pride	hard work	relentlessness	consistency
integrity	tenacity	desire to learn	respect for the game
confidence	love of the game	commitment	

We won't go in to each of these in depth, but three characteristics are particularly important: fun and enjoyment, respect for the game, and taking pride in what you do.

1) Fun and Enjoyment

These two, in one form or another, are required. If you don't enjoy coming to the ballpark, your chances of excelling in baseball are minimal. It doesn't have to be the laughing and smiling enjoyment that you see all the time in the A's Dave Henderson — catching a routine fly ball seems to bring

> *"If you have fun it changes all the pressure into pleasure."*
> *— Ken Griffey Sr.*

him great joy — but if you're going to be good, you've got to be getting some positive emotion from playing the game.

People like to do things they enjoy and avoid things they don't enjoy or cause them pain. To be the best baseball player you can, associate practicing and playing baseball with positive emotions.

Feelings of enjoyment, fun, love and passion for what you are out there doing provide many of the mental skills needed to play well. Positive emotions give you energy, make it easy to concentrate, keep you relaxed and help you feel confident. These positive emotions are the hallmark of a heads-up player.

> *"Sometimes you have to say to yourself that you're going to have fun and feel good before you go out there. Normally, you have fun after you do well, but I wanted to have fun before I did well and that helped."*
> *— Dave Winfield,*
> *member 3,000 Hits Club*

2) Respect for the Game

Respect for the game is commonly found among the best players. Chances are, the players you respect the most have the most respect for baseball. Respecting the game encompasses many things and shows up in a variety of ways.

A player who respects baseball recognizes that the game is difficult and is committed to improving his skills. He works hard in the off-season. When asked how he prepared to hit, Hall of Famer Carl Yastrzemski said the off-season prepared him mentally. "I hated to do weights, I hated to run, I hated to do things and not face a pitcher. But I did them. I swung a lead bat and hit balls — 300-400 a day — into a net for one reason: to toughen myself mentally."

> A player who respects the game emphasizes the quality of his practices. He can't expect to do in a game anything he hasn't done in practice. He can't just "turn it on" and focus in a game if he hasn't done that in practice. Without quality practice there is nothing to "turn on" when the game starts.

Players who respect the game play with intensity. They run out every ground ball — even if it's hit right back to the pitcher — and expect every fly ball to drop. They hustle to back up every play they can on defense. They know what they are supposed to do in different situations and succeed because they have worked hard in practice.

In short, a player who respects the game recognizes that there are no little things in baseball. The slightest edge can make the difference between being safe or out at first base. That runner might score a run and that run might be the difference in the game. It's clear that **EVERYTHING IS A BIG THING.** The player who respects the game makes "extra things" such as good nutritional habits, picking the brains of older players and studying video tape of himself part of his normal routine.

> *"Sometimes when I consider what great consequences come from little things, I am tempted to think that there are no little things."*
> *— Bruce Barton*

3) Pride

This is a key issue for the best players. Pete Rose, one of baseball's most tenacious players, attributed his consistency to one thing: pride. Hitting greats such as Hank Aaron, Stan Musial, Tony Oliva and Rod Carew give the same answer. The pride they took in their hitting was a primary motivator for the daily hard work which led to their amazing consistency.

A strong sense of pride in your baseball performance motivates you to prepare for each practice and game and to play above your physical feelings. If you know you are going to ask yourself when you walk off the field: "Am I proud of what I did today?" you'll probably put forth the extra effort to get the most out of that day.

> Base your pride on how you approached the game or practice, not just the outcome. As a hitter, don't look at it as: "I was 0-for-4. I'm not proud of that." As a pitcher, you might ask: "How can I be proud of a game that I lost?" Outcomes are important but the place you have control is in the **PROCESS** of playing the game. Base your evaluations on how well you "worked the process."

Exercise: What Type of Player Do You Want to Be?

Keeping in mind the importance of a mission and the characteristics involved, use the following questions and statements to clarify your thinking and get at the issue of what type of player you want to be. Some questions may seem repetitive, but fill them out anyway. If you are answering the same way each time, it's a good indication of what you think is important.

If you are committed to becoming a better baseball player, take the time to write out the answers in the space provided in the book or in your journal. There's a big difference between players who are just interested in improving and players who are committed.

Reread the first paragraph in this chapter. What would you like him to talk about?

_____

_____

_____

_____

_____

What do you enjoy about the game?

_____

_____

_____

_____

_____

If you were told this was the last season you were going to be able to play baseball, what attitude would you choose to take each day?

_____

_____

_____

_____

_____

_____

What attitudes displayed by other players impress you the most?

_____

_____

_____

_____

_____

Whom do you consider to be the ideal baseball player?

_____

_____

_____

What makes you feel that way about him?

_____

_____

_____

What moments have given you the greatest satisfaction in baseball? What made them so satisfying?

_____

_____

_____

I'd like to be known as the type of player who:

_____

_____

_____

_____

When I retire I'd like to be able to look back on my career and say:

_____

_____

_____

After reviewing your answers, answer our original question: What type of player would you like to be?

_____

_____

_____

_____

What Would You Like To Accomplish In Baseball?

The answers to this question are called outcomes because they are based on the results of your actions rather than how you go about getting them. When players set goals they usually think of outcomes such as making it to the big leagues, starting for a college team, setting school records, batting .300 or keeping an earned run average below 3.20.

Trying to get the most out of each day is enough for some players, but having specific goals in mind can be very helpful. A clear vision of where you want to end up makes it more likely that you'll get there, whether you're talking about your career or a trip in your car!

To get clear on what you want to accomplish in baseball, respond to the following series of questions. While writing, remember the following guidelines:

1) Have a dream. Players who get the most out of their ability not only have a dream that motivates them, but dream about reaching it regularly. **What you spend your time thinking about often happens.** If you don't think about accomplishing your dream or see yourself not accomplishing your dream, you'll probably fall short of it.

2) Make your goals specific and measurable. A goal motivates you to play at a higher level. But it won't help you unless you know if you've reached it or not. Specific goals create clearer images of what you want to accomplish. The more clearly you see a goal being reached, the more likely you are to reach it.

Whenever you set a goal, ask yourself how you'll know when you've reached it. Statistical goals such as on-base percentage or innings pitched are measured easily. You may have to be more creative, however, if your goal is "to be dedicated" for the season. A way to measure dedication is to first define what dedication means to you and list some things that a dedicated player does. Throughout the season, rate yourself each week on a 1-to-10 scale to see how well you did those things.

3) Make your goals difficult but attainable. Make your goals something you have to stretch for and not easily reached. But don't overdue it. A goal that seems unreachable doesn't motivate and can dampen your spirits instead of exciting them. Your goals should be "realistic," but only you can know what a realistic goal for you is.

4) State your goals in a positive way. Your goals should project the outcomes you want to achieve, not those you want to avoid. It's better to say, "I want to be a dedicated player this year," instead of, "I don't want to be a goof-off this season." Or, instead of, "I don't want to go 2-0 on more than three batters each game," focus on, "I'll throw a strike on one of the first two pitches 90 percent of the time."

5) Adjust your goals when necessary. Change a goal if you achieve it or it becomes clear you can't reach it. If you miss 25 percent of the season because of an injury, adjust goals that were based on your playing the whole season. But if you reach your goal of getting 50 at bats after half the season, it's also time to set a new goal.

Exercise: What Would You Like to Accomplish in Baseball?

Keeping these guidelines in mind, answer the following questions:

What is/are your dream goals for your baseball career?

_____

_____

_____

What is/are your more "realistic" goals for your career?

_____

_____

_____

What are your goals for this season?

_____

_____

_____

What are your goals for this week?

_____

_____

If you don't accomplish these goals, would you be able to like yourself as a person? Why?

_____

_____

_____

_____

To Accomplish Your Goals: Be Present

Lifetime .331 hitter and Hall of Famer Stan Musial said this about his goals: "I set my sights on 200 hits a year. I knew if I was going to get 200 hits I was going to be scoring runs, driving in runs and moving guys around. That was my goal. I didn't look at my statistics every week or two weeks, though. When the All-Star game came around I'd look around and see how I was doing, where I stood, and I'd go from there."

Musial had a long-term goal, but his daily focus was on the process of hitting: "My idea of hitting was to get the fat part of the bat on the ball and hit it where it was pitched, and that's basically what I was trying to do."

No matter what outcome you'd like to achieve, once you've chosen a direction to go, the relevant question is, "How do I get there?"

Let's take the example of hitting .300. Hitting .300 takes a lot of hits and to get them you need to consistently hit the ball hard. You must have quality at bats in which you feel confident, are in control of yourself, see the ball and make good swings on good pitches. You need to be totally focused on one pitch at a time.

> Once again, we're back to the ingredients necessary for playing good baseball, to the present moment and the process of playing the game. There may be a goal you are trying to reach in the future, but the present is the only place where you have any degree of control. What you accomplish in a season is really the sum of all your present moments, and what you accomplish in your career is really the sum of all of your "todays."

YOUR CAREER = TODAY + TODAY + TODAY + TODAY + ...

Your present approach to the game is where to place the emphasis of your mission. Focus more on the "how" than the "what," on the process more than the outcome.

Putting Your Mission into Action on a Daily Basis

You've clarified your mission by deciding why you play baseball, what type of player you want to be, and what you'd like to accomplish in the game, and you realize the present moment is where the action is. Let's finish this chapter by examining how to put your mission into action each day.

"Each day you get to make a choice whether you are going to take a step forward, remain the same, or take a step back."
— Kirk McCaskill

Each day is a mini-career. Saying "I'll get committed tomorrow," or "I'll do extra work later in the week," won't help you find

Frank Thomas appears to be on a mission each time he comes to the plate.

out how good you can be (and the person talking about you at your retirement banquet isn't going to say the things you want to hear).

You can't retire and say you got the most out of your ability if you don't get the most out of it today. If you want to say you're proud of your playing career after you re-

> *"The time is now, the place is here."*
> — **Dan Millman**

tire, make it today's mission to conduct yourself in a way that makes you proud.

A clear mission gives you perspective, direction, intensity, and meaning, and opens the door to your learning as much as possible. In addition, it helps avoid the "Going-Through-The-Motions" mind-set that cripples many players and keeps them from finding out how good they can be. In essence, your mission becomes your attitude. It's a decision you make on a day-to-day basis.

It's a simple process to put your mission into action on a daily basis:

1) Ask yourself before each game or practice, "What is today's mission?" or "What do I want to get out of today?"

2) Keep that mission in mind as you play the game or work through the practice.

3) Ask yourself at the end of the day, "How did I do on today's mission?"

Keep your answer to "What is today's mission?" short and simple. One mission a day is plenty. Avoid having more than three in a day. Here are some possible "mini-missions:"

"Today's mission is to...

- *be a cocky, confident player."*
- *work on my prepitch routine during batting practice."*
- *keep my hands relaxed on all ground balls."*
- *work hard."*
- *listen to my coach."*
- *have fun playing baseball."*
- *respect the game of baseball."*
- *work on ground balls to my right."*
- *support my teammates."*
- *have a positive attitude."*
- *see how much I can learn."*
- *be relentless."*
- *project an image of self-confidence."*
- *take 50 swings off the tee hitting the ball to the opposite field."*

These are a few examples of missions you can set for yourself each day. Your answers to the questions about what type of player you'd like to be are an endless supply of mini-missions. Review your answers once a week to help keep you on track. You may have the same mission every day for a week or every day for an entire season — that's OK as long as the mission has meaning for you.

At the end of each day, grade yourself A through F or rate yourself on a 1-to-10 scale on how successful you were at accomplishing your mission.

Accomplishing a mission you have set builds your confidence. It's like making a deposit in a bank account that you can draw on whenever you need it. In time, you build a reputation with yourself that says, "I'm a guy who does what he sets out to do." Confidence and mental toughness are built one day at a time.

The Coach's Box

Coaches can incorporate the daily mission idea by asking players to set a team mission at the start of practice or before a game. The mission could be to be focused all day, to make it an intense practice or to talk only about baseball the whole session. They almost always come up with something good. You may also want to ask them how you'll know they're accomplishing their mission.

At the end of practice, ask the players to rate or grade themselves on how well they accomplished that mission. Be sure to ask for specific examples of when the mission was being done well and when it was being done poorly.

Taking Control

3

First baseman Jim Stevens moved 5 feet to his right to get in front of a ground ball. All he has to do is field the ball and step on first to end the inning.

Although he's in good position to make the play, Jim suddenly stiffens, raising his glove off the ground allowing the ball to skip between his legs and the runner on third to score easily.

As Jim holds the runner on first, his mind reruns the missed play. After two weeks of sitting on the bench he finally gets a chance to play and blows a simple ground ball. More thoughts start going through his mind; the game seems to be moving faster and faster. "We would have been out of the inning if it hadn't been for me," he thinks to himself. "How could I do that after all the extra ground balls I've been taking in practice? I'll bet my parents are really embarrassed. I can forget playing again for awhile..."

Jim won't look to see his coach's reaction. He doesn't need to — he feels the anger radiating from the dugout. He feels empty and shaky inside, and he's out of balance. "Please, don't let the next ball come to me," he thinks to himself. "Let's just get out of this inning."

Jim has lost control. If the next play does come his way, he'll be shaky at best. Most players have had the same feelings and know it isn't much fun.

Confidence is the goal of the mental game. If you're not in control of yourself, you aren't playing with confidence. With all those thoughts and feelings running wild, you aren't playing the game one pitch at a time. It's your responsibility to be in control of yourself. To consistently play at or near your best, you need to understand a few things about self-control that will help develop your ability to control yourself on the field.

Two Fundamentals

This chapter deals with two fundamental ideas on control which form the foundation for playing baseball one pitch at a time:

1) You can't control what happens around you, but you can control how you choose to respond.

2) You must be in control of yourself before you can control your performance.

The deep breath, a simple but powerful tool that you can use to help put these two ideas into action, will be explained at the end of this chapter.

Control Point No. 1 — *You can't control what happens around you, but you can control how you choose to respond*

Below is a list of factors that can affect the outcome of a game. Circle the factors over which you, as a player, have control.

• an umpire's call	• field conditions	• your attitude
• the crowd	• your teammates' performances	
• your effort	• your coach	• luck
• the weather	• your opponent's ability	
• you getting a hit	• getting a batter out (as pitcher)	

The pattern should be obvious. The only thing you can control is yourself. Realizing this point played a critical role in the success of two-time Cy Young Award winner Greg Maddux.

"Other than my at bats, I have no control over the runs we're going to score," said Maddux. "But I can control the pitches I make, how I handle my mechanics, how I control my frame of mind. That's what benefited me most. I can't control what happens outside of my pitching."

You can't control whether you get a base hit or get a batter out. If you've ever smashed a line drive right at a fielder or thrown a great pitch that went for a base hit, you know that you can do everything right and still "fail."

Greg Maddux says understanding that the only things he can control are himself and his pitches has been critical to his success.

But energy spent worrying about what is outside of your control takes away from the energy needed to focus on your performance. Baseball is hard enough the way it is. Don't play it with part of your brain tied behind your back.

The diagram below, adapted from Steven Covey, illustrates this idea. The area inside the large circle is everything that is a concern to you. The area inside the small circle is everything you can control.

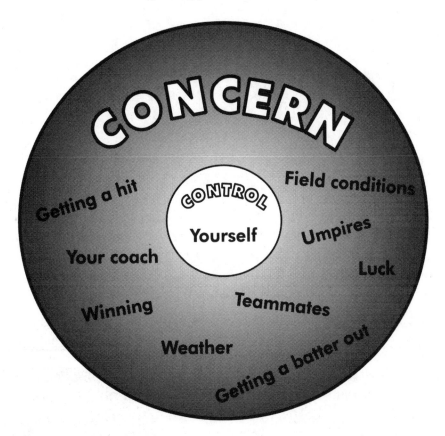

The "circle of concern" for hitters includes getting a base hit, umpires' calls, conditions in the batter's box, the ability and positioning of the defense and the pitch you are thrown. The area of concern for pitchers includes getting the batter out, a defense that makes the plays behind you and getting a win. The defense is concerned with how the ball is hit, the hops it takes off the ground and the performance of teammates.

But all of these things are only "concerns." They are not within your control. The only thing in your "circle of control" is yourself.

The illustrations on the following page demonstrate the effects of thinking about things outside of your control.

A hitter who has had two hits in his last 23 at bats is represented on the left. He's got all kinds of thoughts on his mind. Any that aren't aimed at things he can control are getting in his way. On the right is the mind of a hitter who is in control of himself. His thoughts are clear and focused on the only thing that's important right now — the ball.

Focus your energies on the things you can control if you want to be the best player you can. Understand that the outcome of a game, what your teammates do, the way your opponent plays, and the decisions of your coach or general manager are concerns of yours, but don't spend a lot of energy thinking about them because they are outside of your control.

Choose Your Response

Because you can't control what happens to or around you, it's critical to realize that you can control the way you respond to what happens. You **can choose how you respond to any situation on or off the field.**

Imagine you've been playing poorly. You've had three straight bad outings on the mound, you're 0-for-your-last-10 at bats or you just made an error that cost your team two runs. How do you feel? What are your thoughts about yourself? How do you carry yourself physically?

Most people would walk around the field with their heads down, thinking bad thoughts about themselves and wondering what will go wrong next. You're clearly not playing heads-up baseball! But is there anything in these situations that really **makes** you feel this way?

One of the great things about being a human is the ability to think independently of our surroundings. For instance, you can choose at any time to recall your greatest pitches or best hits. Do this for a few minutes and you'll start to feel pretty good. Our minds don't do a good job of differentiating between what is real and what is imagined (see Imagery in the Appendix for more on this idea), so seeing yourself succeeding over and over is a good confidence builder.

The best players spend a lot of time thinking about playing well. In fact, choosing to think about playing well plays a part in these players' success. They play great largely because they think about playing great.

Recalling your failures and replaying them over and over can cause an opposite reaction. Doing that raises doubts about your ability to play baseball. Prolonging this negative state of mind results in poor play, reinforcing your negative thinking.

> What you choose to think about largely determines how you play, so choose your thinking wisely. **CHOOSE TO THINK ABOUT PLAYING WELL!**

Mentally tough players make good choices about what they think about. They take responsibility for their thinking and choose to think effective, helpful thoughts in all situations rather than simply letting what goes on around them determine their thoughts. Allowing yourself to feel down or upset during adversity and only feel confident when everything is going your way puts you on an emotional roller coaster — you'll be going up and down as success comes and goes. You can't afford that kind of ride if you want to be the best ballplayer you can! Besides, you want to go to the ballpark every day, not the amusement park.

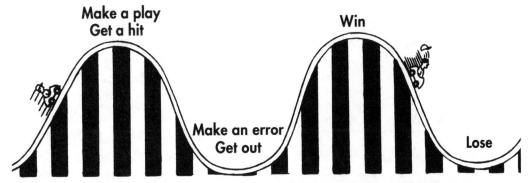

Failing to take responsibility for your thinking can make the ballpark seem more like an amusement park.

It's difficult to think positively when your performances aren't what you wanted. It's natural for hitters to question themselves when they fail to get a hit in eight or nine at bats. Falling short of expectations in any part of the game often leads to negative feelings such as anger, frustration, tension and doubt. If you don't really know what you want to be thinking and don't consciously choose what to think, your thoughts are left to chance. Sometimes they're good, sometimes they're bad. Sounds like a recipe for inconsistency, doesn't it? The heads-up player **CHOOSES** what to think about instead of leaving his thoughts — which largely determine how he plays — to **CHANCE.**

Keeping your thoughts positive in the face of failure is difficult. Negative reactions to bad things are natural so more than likely it's become a habit and changing a habit is tough. If you've ever tried to change your mechanics, quit chewing tobacco or learn a new position, you've found developing new habits takes time and repetition — mindful repetition, not just going through the motions. Make effective thinking a habit so that your thoughts naturally become proactive, confident and performance enhancing.

So point No. 1 about control is that you can't control what happens around you, but you can control your reaction to it if you take responsibility for your thinking. Understanding this intellectually is one thing, understanding it emotionally, which is where it needs to be, is another, so we'll keep reminding you of it.

Control Point No. 2 — *You Must Be in Control of Yourself Before You Can Control Your Performance*

When you are "in control of yourself" you are composed, thinking clearly and confidently, and aware of what is happening both inside and outside of you. Your movements are fluid and you feel centered and balanced. Adrenaline may be pumping or you feel anxious, but you are able to focus that energy in a way that helps instead of hurts your performance. In short, you are in control of yourself when you are composed.

"A pitcher can't control his pitches unless he's in control of himself."
— Gene Mauch, former major-league manager

Self-control goes hand-in-hand with confidence. In the terms we used to describe confidence, having control of yourself means that you remove obstacles such as tension, doubt and fears about what might happen in the future. Only then are you "free" to trust yourself and allow your natural abilities and skills to shine through.

Unfortunately, players' minds are often cluttered and the game seems to move into fast-forward. They can't make good decisions and struggle to play up to their capabilities. This can cause batters to swing at bad pitches, pitchers to "rush" in their delivery and fielders to make errors.

Picture firemen using a hose to put out a fire. Water is very effective on fire, but forcefully pumping water through the hose only helps if the firemen have control of the hose and can focus the spray on the fire! If they lose control of the hose, the pressure from the water makes the hose writhe wildly like a crazed snake and no homes will be saved.

It's the same with your natural ability and the skills you develop in practice. They're of no use unless you control yourself and focus your mental "spray" where it needs to be. Pressure can cause you to revert to old habits, wiping out hours you've spent working on your game.

Learning to recognize when this is happening can save time in the future and get you back on your game more quickly. For example, problems such as a batter pulling his shoulder off the ball or a pitcher changing his arm slot are often misdiagnosed as "mechanical" problems resulting in a great deal of time spent drilling the proper technique. Drilling mechanics is important, but the new mechanics aren't going to show up if a player can't control himself on the field. If the player normally has sound mechanics, these are not mechanical problems, they are thinking problems.

If you aren't in control of your mind, you can't control your body. Marcel Lachemann, longtime pitching coach and now manager of the California Angels, explains what happens when pitchers aren't in control of themselves:

California Angels manager Marcel Lachemann, left, feels many "mechanical" problems are actually the result of a player losing control of himself mentally.

Most guys lose control of themselves before they lose control of their mechanics. When a player breaks down mechanically early in a game or tight situation, it usually isn't because of fatigue. Their mechanics break down because they've lost control of themselves. They panic, even at the major-league level. It can be caused by anything from an umpire blowing a call, an error by a teammate or a guy getting a hit. You can see their mechanics break down: their delivery speeds up, they change their arm slots, they lose their balance, they stop throwing strikes. Those are all losses of mental control.

> Developing the ability to control yourself in the heat of battle is an essential component of playing heads-up baseball. When you are in control, all other aspects of playing well, such as making good decisions and using your best mechanics, become easier. The player who is under control is playing the game one pitch at a time. He's not upset about something that happened on a previous pitch or worried about what might happen on a future pitch. His focus is on the present pitch. That's where he has control.

A Slow, Steady Breath:
The Mental Game's Most Versatile Skill

One of the easiest yet most powerful skills to help gain and keep self-control is a deep breath. Stopping to take a slow, steady breath serves a number of purposes, and many players find it to be the most helpful mental game skill they learn.

Try it right now. While reading, take a good breath. Place one hand on your stomach and take a long, slow, deep breath. Let the breath push your hand away from your spine. Don't expand your chest or raise your shoulders much as you inhale. Think of drawing the air into your stomach as the belly is gently pushed out. When comfortably full of air, relax, and allow the air to flow out of you as the belly moves in.

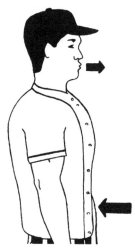

Take two more breaths the same way. This time, scan your body for tension as you inhale. As you exhale, let the excess tension go and feel yourself (especially your shoulders) sink down slightly into whatever you are sitting or lying on.

You probably discovered you were tensing muscles that didn't need to be tensed, so you let them relax. Excess tension is a major obstacle to great performance. The breath can help free you of the tension and allow you to play your best baseball.

The deep breath is the mental game's most versatile player because it can be used almost any time for almost any purpose. Below are some of the main uses for the breath. Each will be covered again as you move through the book.

A good breath:

1) Puts your focus on the present moment. When you are playing one pitch at a time you are totally focused on what is going on right now instead of thinking about what happened in the past or might happen in the future. Focusing on your breath helps you concentrate on the present moment because your breath is coming in and out right now!

2) Enables you to "check in" with yourself to see if you are in control. If you can't get yourself to take a deep breath it may be because your mind is going too fast to remember to do it or you're too tight to get the air in. This is a good indicator that you aren't in control and that you need to take an extra moment — and an extra breath — to get centered and balanced before the next pitch. We'll talk more about the importance of "checking in" during the next chapter.

Taking quality breaths on the mound has helped Jim Abbott play the game one pitch at a time.

3) Helps you get control. We've talked a lot about how the game seems to speed up when you aren't in control. A deep breath helps you slow it down. Be sure you don't rush the breath. A short, shallow, rapid breath in which the air only gets into the upper part of your chest won't do nearly as much good as a long, slow, deep one that fills your abdomen.

The term "choke" is derived from the fact that nervousness often makes the muscles in our shoulders, neck and chest tighten, resulting in short, shallow and rapid breathing. This leads to other muscles tightening up. Making a conscious effort to breathe deeply and fully helps you relax and directly counters the conditions that lead to "choking" on the field.

4) Helps release negatives. When something bad happens it usually leads to cluttered thinking (as in the drawing), tense muscles, or, in most cases, both. Remember, you can't control what happens to you, but you can choose how you respond to it. Respond with a breath! As you exhale, think of "blowing off" those last two pitches you threw that bounced in the dirt, the swing you took at a pitch over your head, the fly ball you misjudged, or any negative thing that just happened. A breath can blow that "monkey" off your back.

5) Energizes you when you are feeling sluggish. When you are feeling too relaxed or "flat," taking a breath that really emphasizes the inhalation can help you get energized. A short series of hard, fast breaths accompanied by a pump-up talk to yourself and a few sprints can help you snap out of the listless funk where baseball players often find themselves after they've been on the field for a few hours (or a few minutes!).

6) Helps you shift from conscious thinking to "unconscious" trusting. When a player is playing well his teammates often say he's "unconscious." A breath immediately before a pitch can help you make the transition between conscious preparation (such as planning what pitch to throw) and unconscious performance. As you exhale, think of sending your focus out at your target and moving into a state of trust where you let yourself perform freely rather than trying hard.

7) Helps establish a sense of rhythm in your pitching, hitting or fielding. Good players have a rhythm or tempo in their motions. Unfortunately, most players wait, hoping they'll fall into a rhythm. Instead, choose to use your breath to help you get into a tempo before each pitch. Most coaching is focused on establishing rhythm during the pitch, but the best place to establish rhythm is between pitches.

A good, slow, steady breath can do many things for you and can serve many purposes at the same time — we aren't talking about taking seven breaths between each pitch! In the next chapter, we will give you some ideas on how using the breath between pitches will help you play the game one pitch at a time.

Breathing Exercises

Each of these exercises helps develop the skill of controlling yourself on the field. Like any physical skill, you only get better at it with practice.

1) At least five times during each of the next five days, pause for a moment and take one or two good breaths. Focus on the air as it comes in to your abdomen and feel yourself relax as you exhale. Be aware of how your body feels after each breath.

2) To experience the benefits of the breath, use it while stretching before a game or practice. During any stretching exercise, take a good breath and allow yourself to relax and sink further into the stretch as you exhale. For example, when bending at the waist to stretch your hamstrings, take a deep breath and let it out easily. Let go of your tension and allow your upper body to move closer to your feet. Don't force this action, just relax and let yourself go. Repeat the breath and allow yourself to sink even further into the stretch.

3) Lie on your back in a quiet place. Make yourself comfortable and begin taking slow, steady, deep breaths from your abdomen. Think "inhale" as your stomach rises from the air you draw in. Think of the number of the breath you are letting go as you relax and allow the air to flow out of your abdomen. Repeat to yourself, "inhale... one ... inhale... two .... inhale ... three..." and so forth. When you reach 10, count backwards to zero and begin again. See if you can make it to 10 without letting any thoughts other than your breath and your counting take over your mind. Play with this exercise for five minutes or so each day or every other day for awhile, then progress up to 20 minutes.

In a game, you need to concentrate on the next pitch so fully that all other thoughts are blocked out. This exercise helps develop that ability. In the game, nothing matters except the next pitch; in this exercise tell yourself that nothing matters except the next breath.

The Coach's Box

Coach, watch your players to see who is in control. If you know they are supposed to be taking breaths between pitches and you don't see it happening, you know they aren't focusing on their mental games. Long Beach State coach Dave Snow found this to be a very helpful tool that led to an increase in the quality of his practices and the game performances of his players: "I can look around and see who is focused by seeing if they are taking a deep breath — and this is both in practice and in games. If I see guys taking their breaths I know they are clicked in, working their routines, and are at least trying to keep themselves under control. If I don't see guys taking breaths, I know they're not into it or are out of control."

Playing the Game
One Pitch at a Time

George Roberts, a young college pitcher, looked like he had good stuff when he started the game. The first two batters went down easily, but the third hit a decent pitch for an opposite-field home run.

George is shaken. Instead of collecting himself and getting right back into his rhythm, he rapidly begins to lose control and walks the fourth and fifth hitters.

Just trying to get the ball over the plate, George practically lobs the ball to the next two batters who respond with sharp singles to left field making the score 3-0. The eighth hitter flied out to center to end the rally, but an inning that started well for George became a nightmare because he lost control of himself.

He pitched well the rest of the game, but lost 5-3. As is often the case, it wasn't the home run that beat him, his reaction to it did!

You've already learned that you can't control events around you, but you can control your response to them. George couldn't control the batter hitting the home run. He might have been able to throw a better pitch, but even good pitches are hit for home runs sometimes. What he could have done was react more effectively to it.

George didn't play the first inning one pitch at a time. He had good command of his pitches when the inning began, but couldn't keep his composure after the home run. He was mentally replaying that one pitch (and a few others he threw later) the rest of the inning. In effect, he was throwing several pitches at the same time.

If you're a pitcher, try this the next time you're in the bullpen. Put two baseballs in your throwing hand and throw both balls at the same time. Make sure to throw them both for good, low strikes. If you fail, get really upset, add a third ball, and throw all three for strikes. (Make sure your catcher is in full gear!)

Just as you can't accurately throw three baseballs at once, you can't be successful when you let your anger or frustration from one pitch affect your next pitch.

Playing more than one pitch at a time is not a problem unique to pitchers. Hitters often let one pitch throw off an entire at bat. A "bad" call on strike one or strike two, for example, can so upset a batter that he fails to focus on the pitch that actually gets him out. "The umpire took the bat out of my hands," he's likely to complain, not realizing that the bat is only out of his hands when he's called out.

> *"Once my catcher and I determine the pitch, that's all there is. There's nobody standing there then. I don't think about the next game, the next inning, the next hitter, the next play. There's only the next pitch. It's the only job I have."*
> *— Orel Hershiser, Los Angeles Dodgers*

Hitters also frequently let one bad at bat get in the way of another. After making an out or two, hitters begin to try harder with each trip to the plate, "giving away" at bats because they lose control. They try to do too much with each pitch instead of trusting their ability. Slumps happen when hitters come to the plate carrying the weight of several "o-fors" on their backs.

Carrying frustrations from one bat to the next is like trying to hit a three-run homer with no one on base.

Fielders may react the same way after committing an error. Fear, doubt and tension from the error get in the way of making a successful play later in the game. Similarly, defensive players aren't playing the game one pitch at a time if they are thinking about how they just struck out with the bases loaded or, on the other extreme, about what they're going to do after the game!

The Process of Playing One Pitch at a Time

When you play well, you focus totally on each pitch. You are in control of yourself, think clearly and let yourself perform. Only when under control can you think clearly about what to do next, and only when under control can you give up control and get to trust.

Playing the game one pitch at a time consists of three basic steps:

- **Self-control**

- **Plan your performance**

- **Trust yourself**

- **Self-Control.** Turn your focus inward and check in to see what's going on. Are you where you want to be mentally and physically? If so, start planning your performance. If you aren't where you want to be, use your mental skills to make an adjustment. If you are too tense, you need to release the tension. If you are too relaxed or "flat," pick yourself up. Special ways to make these adjustments will be given later in this chapter.
- **Plan Your Performance.** This means deciding what you are going to do. If you're a pitcher, it may mean throwing a fastball low and

away. If you're a hitter, it may mean looking for a pitch on the outside half of the plate and hitting the ball the other way. When you have made your plan, make a commitment to your decision and put your focus on the task at hand.

- **Trust.** Finally, you perform. Trust yourself. Trust your preparation and just do it. Turn control over to your body and let it go. Trust is confidence in action.

When you play well this process happens so rapidly you probably aren't thinking about it. That's what you want. But most players say that only happens about 10 percent of the time. Learning this process in more detail will give you something to go to the other 90 percent of the time.

> *"People who keep it simple the longest are the most successful."*
> — *Kirk McCaskill,*
> *Chicago White Sox*

Remember to keep it simple. There isn't time for a lengthy routine between pitches. Pitchers must work quickly, hitters need to keep the game moving and fielders must be ready for each pitch. The three examples at the end of the chapter will show you how to work through this process in a matter of seconds.

Step 1: Self-control

You are the only thing in a ball game you can control, and you must be in control of yourself before you can control your performance. This makes the question before each pitch, "Am I in control of myself?" For the answer, check in. Checking in is getting feedback from yourself — checking in to see if you are relaxed as you want to be, if you are thinking confident thoughts, if your focus is where it needs to be and if you are clear about what you are trying to do on the next pitch.

Checking in on yourself gives you "awareness." Awareness is like getting feedback from your coach on what, if any, adjustments are necessary to improve your performance. The best players excel at coaching themselves. Rather than rely on their coach, they recognize when adjustments are needed and what adjustments to make.

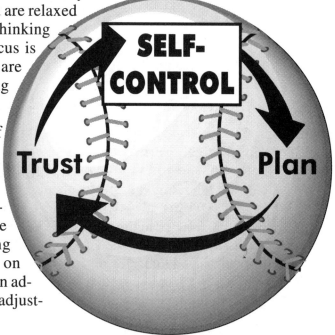

Awareness is Like an Internal Traffic Light

To help you understand awareness, think of it like a traffic light inside your body. When you are driving, a traffic light tells you what to do as you approach a potentially dangerous intersection. Green means "go," continue with what you are doing. Yellow means caution and red means stop. Awareness is different from thinking; it's more like a feeling or sensation. You don't really think as you approach a traffic light in your car; you see the light and respond to it. Likewise, don't think too much when you are playing, just be aware of what is happening and then respond to it.

When you are playing well, your traffic light is green. You're just doing it; you're in the flow or "the zone," and you've got rhythm. Cruise right on through any "intersections" you encounter.

Your yellow light comes on when you start to have trouble. Swinging at a bad pitch, giving up a base hit or seeing your girlfriend with another guy in the stands can throw you slightly off your game. You're a little too tense, you're not quite focused or you're rushing.

You're really struggling when you hit your red light. Maybe you walked two batters, made an error or had the coach yell at you. Your mind is racing. You're tense and shaken and looking forward to the end of the inning or game.

The green-to-yellow-to-red progression is similar to the "spiraling out of control" illustrated earlier. As pictured below, a green light means you are in control; you are "centered and balanced." You are getting off center when the yellow lights comes on, and you're in the early stages of losing control. You've lost control when the red light is on.

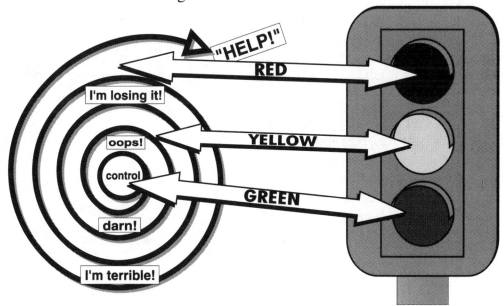

> Learn to recognize when you have a green light and when you don't. Regaining control isn't difficult at the yellow light stage, but when you hit a red light, it becomes much tougher.

Unfortunately, when players sense a yellow light they react the same way most drivers would — they speed up to get through it. This also is a common response to a stressful situation. Players (and coaches) perceive the game going faster and faster, so they go faster and faster to keep up which leads to trouble.

> You can get away with "disobeying" or not seeing your internal traffic light sometimes, but before long you'll end up a major wreck. Crashing and burning isn't much fun. To avoid accidents, see the traffic light as you approach it. If it changes to yellow, keep your composure and make a sound decision about how to react.

Exercise: Getting to Know Your Traffic Lights

To have awareness on the field, think through situations that cause stress and what that stress or pressure causes you to do. Do you rush yourself, tense your hands or shoulders, or try harder, for example? Know in advance where the "intersections" of the game are — those times when you need to check your internal traffic light. The following exercise will help you identify when and where to look for trouble. You can't make the adjustments needed to play consistently and be heads-up if you aren't aware an adjustment is needed.

Write your responses to the questions in each box. Here are some common responses.

Green Light examples:

- I get a green light when:
    - I prepare myself mentally for the game
    - I have a good at bat
    - I get a good batter out
    - I use my routine

- When I have a green light, I feel:
    - Energized, excited, calm, relaxed
    - Totally focused on the baseball
    - The target I'm throwing to looks big and close

- When I have a green light, I say to myself:
    Nothing
    "I'm unstoppable"
    "Hit the ball to me"

Yellow Light examples:

- I get a yellow light when:
    I can't commit to my plan
    I swing at a bad pitch
    The umpire blows a call
    I make an error

- When I have a yellow light, I feel:
    The game speed up, I think of a million things
    Tightness in my shoulders and the backs of my legs
    I start to try harder
    Upset

- When I have a yellow light, I say to myself:
    "I'm losing it"
    "Here we go again"
    "Why does this always happen to me?"

Red Light examples:

- I get a red light when:
    I have two yellow lights in a row
    I'm 0 for my last 6 at bats
    I give up a home run
    I make a stupid error

- When I have a red light, I feel:
    My jaw clench tightly
    Enraged
    Like quitting
    Myself throw my equipment

- When I have a red light, I say to myself:
    #%*&@!$&*%!@!!
    "Why do I play this stupid game?"
    "I'm a loser"

RED LIGHTS
When do you get them?

What do you feel?

What do you say to yourself?

GREEN LIGHTS
When do you get them?

What do you feel?

What do you say to yourself?

HITTING

YELLOW LIGHTS
When do you get them?

What do you feel?

What do you say to yourself?

PITCHING/DEFENSE

RED LIGHTS
When do you get them?

What do you feel?

What do you say to yourself?

GREEN LIGHTS
When do you get them?

What do you feel?

What do you say to yourself?

YELLOW LIGHTS
When do you get them?

What do you feel?

What do you say to yourself?

Now you know when and where to look for signals that tell you whether you need to make an adjustment to get yourself under control. Make it a habit to look for them during practice so you'll be able to spot them during games.

Skills for Gaining Control

When you have a green light, go ahead and simply play the game. But when you recognize a yellow or red light approaching, it's time to make an adjustment to get back to green or back to the center of the spiral. Here are some simple techniques you can use to do that.

1) Recognize when You Aren't in Control

Recognizing you aren't in control of yourself and that you're not relaxed and focused is often enough to get you back to where you want to be. Watch for "intersections" in the game where a yellow light could pop up.

2) Use Your Breath

Taking a breath is a powerful tool for gaining control. Take a good breath right now; relax your body as you exhale. Where were you tense? That's the first place to look when you have a yellow light in a game.

3) Take Some Time

Time can be one of your best friends. A great thing about baseball is that you can take a short walk, tie your shoe laces, or whatever between pitches to help you get settled down.

4) Use a Release

Develop a routine or gesture to symbolically "release" or let go of negative thoughts and feelings. The basic idea is simple. Pick up some dirt, a rock, some grass, the rosin bag, or whatever object you choose. Put your anger or frustration into it by squeezing it. Then throw the object away telling yourself that you are throwing away the last pitch, the error you made or whatever is annoying you. You need to put your negative emotions somewhere; put them into something you can throw out of your way.

> *"If I give up a home run I wipe my foot across the rubber and clean it off. Now the slate is clean. It's a new batter, a new situation."*
> — **Mark Langston, California Angels**

Another way to release a negative is to wipe it out of your mind. Pitchers can use a foot to wipe dirt from the pitching rubber to "wipe away their anger" over something they just did. Then they can focus on the next pitch with a clean slate. Hitters can clear out something that has them upset by smoothing the batter's box before they step in. Infielders can smooth footprints in the dirt to clean up after an error.

Taking some extra time, left, or "wiping away" a negative, right, can help you regain control.

You aren't a robot; it's OK to be a little upset when you make a mistake or catch a bad break. Develop a routine to use when you run into a yellow or red light. Take off your hat or glove, or your mask if you're a catcher, when something goes wrong. When your hat or glove is off it's your time to be upset or depressed. But when you put it back on it's time to focus on this next pitch. Don't put your glove or hat back on until you have let go of whatever happened and are ready to focus on the next pitch. Finally, you can release a negative by simply turning your back to home plate. When you turn around to face the plate, everything is positive.

In short, develop a physical action that helps you turn negative thoughts into positive ones.

5) Pick a Focal Point

Many players pick a focal point in the ballpark before a game begins that helps them gain control during the game. It could be a sign, a flag, a place on the outfield fence or anything else you know will be there throughout the game. Make it something that reminds you of all the work you've put in to get where you are today. When you look at it during a game, it reminds you that you've paid your dues and you're ready to perform. It reminds you to play the game one pitch at a time and to focus on the ingredients of playing baseball.

Take a moment to look at your focal point when you need a boost during the ball game (when you have a yellow or red light). If it's a powerful symbol that really speaks to you, it will help you get things together.

6) Carry Yourself to Confidence

You can tell when a player has lost confidence or control of himself by the way he carries himself. Hitters in a dry spell often shuffle around with their shoulders hunched, heads down and chests sunken. This is probably where the term slump came from!

> A simple and effective way to regain control is to carry yourself as if you were extremely confident and in control. Thinking confident thoughts makes you feel confident; carrying yourself in a confident way does the same thing.

Dennis Eckersley, whose records set as a closer have earned him a reputation as "The Man" in the Oakland Athletics bullpen, uses this approach when he comes in and doesn't feel like "The Man:"

"You fake it. You do. The next thing you know, it works. You can't let on that you're not throwing well. There's a body language; I really believe it. You've still got to act like you're the man. You can't fake a good fastball, I'm not saying that, but you have to give the impression that your stuff is on time."

Dennis Eckersley

To understand the power of this idea, try this exercise: slump down in your chair like you're depressed after making the error that cost your team the game. Get your head down, lower your shoulders and breathe very slowly. Read the following:

> *"You are a loser. I can't believe you screwed up that play. All you had to do was catch the ball and the inning would have been over. You're brutal. You can't play this game so why do you even try? Why don't you just quit? Hang it up. You can't do anything right and you never have, so why bother?"*

Depressing, isn't it? If you got into it at all, you probably started believing it. "Yeah, he's right. Maybe I should quit."

Now sit up or stand up straight and tall. Take a good, deep breath, lift your sternum and hold your head proudly like you are the most confident guy you've ever seen. Remain in that position and read the passage again.

> To carry yourself more like a heads-up player, try the following suggestions:
> - Keep your head up.
> - Lift your sternum (chest bone).
> - Act like the most confident player you know.
> - Think about your greatest performance and carry yourself the way you did that day.
> - Create space between your pelvis and rib cage.

Was there a difference? People often find that the words seem to bounce off if they are carrying themselves confidently. The words don't get to them as they did when they were slouched over and depressed.

Project an image that says, "I'm in control" regardless of how you feel. You might not match the intensity of Dave Stewart's eyes or the presence Kirby Puckett has at the plate, but it helps to try.

Experiment with these skills for gaining control so you have something to go to when you start spiraling out of control. There's no guarantee they will get you back to center, but they can give you your best chance of playing one pitch at a time.

Step 2: Plan Your Performance

Once you have a green light or come as close as you can in the time you have between pitches, develop a plan for what you are trying to accomplish on the next pitch. Think of it as having a mission for each pitch. The two basic requirements for a good plan: make it simple, make it clear.

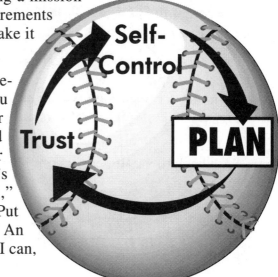

Chances of accomplishing something increase if you know what you are trying to do! Plans for a pitcher might be: "Curveball, low and away," "Fastball, up and in," or "Change-up, hit the mitt." A hitter's plan might be: "Hit the fastball," "Drive the ball to right center," or "Put the fat part of the bat on the ball." An infielder might think: "Turn two if I can, if not get the sure out."

There's no need to get complicated. If you do, you're asking for trouble.

Before deciding on a plan for a given pitch, do some thinking about your strategy. For hitters, use the information you have on the pitcher. This comes from when you've faced him before, from what you've seen him throw to other batters and from what you've been told about the guy. Then come up with a plan for what pitch you are looking to hit. Maybe you're going to sit on a fastball, wait for an off-speed pitch or simply, "see the ball, hit the ball."

How much thinking and guessing you are comfortable doing is up to you. The main thing is to have a clear idea of what you are doing up there. Don't give away at bats because you didn't have a mission.

Pitchers deciding on a strategy should think through how to pitch to the batter. Base your strategy on your abilities and the information you've collected about the hitter. Catchers will think along the same lines, and other players will decide where to position themselves. The goal is to come up with a simple and clear plan for the pitch.

This is why having yourself under control is critical. If you aren't under control, you can't think clearly about what to do on the next pitch.

Commit to the Plan

> This point can't be emphasized enough. **COMMIT TO THE PLAN YOU DECIDE ON.** This is a critical component of playing heads-up baseball and playing the game one pitch at a time.

Recall the pitcher who starts his windup with one pitch in mind only to wonder halfway through his windup if he should be throwing a different one. He lacks commitment. The "wrong" pitch thrown with commitment is much more effective than the "right" pitch thrown with doubt.

Hitters face the same dilemma. Planning to hit the ball up the middle doesn't help if you end up trying to pull the ball out of the park once the pitch is on its way. That usually results in a swing and a miss or a weak ground ball. For a hitter, failure to commit to a plan is an out.

An attempt to steal a base without being committed has the same result — a free trip back to the dugout.

Visualize the Plan

Seeing yourself executing your plan before the pitch is thrown strengthens your commitment and sharpens your concentration. If you can, see it happen in your mind, then do it for real. If you can't visualize any part of the pitch, don't worry about it.

Pitcher Bert Blyleven, a 273-game winner explains how visualization was vital to his success:

"Visualization is concentration. Once I know what I want to throw, I visualize that pitch before I actually throw it. I visualize, for example, a fastball low and away. I don't necessarily see the whole flight of the ball, but I see in my mind the ball traveling the last 2 or 3 feet or so before it hits the glove. Then it's a matter of executing what I just visualized."

The best defensive players often visualize balls being hit to them during the time between pitches. This gives them a chance to rehearse their plan and sharpen their focus. Hitters can lock themselves into their plan by seeing themselves driving the ball up the middle or hitting a curveball to the opposite field. Your mind stays focused on whatever it visualizes.

Visualizing just before the pitch helps "block out" all other distractions. Coaches and teammates often tell players to "block out the fans," "block out that error you made," "block out the fact that you've struck out on your last three trips to the plate," or "block all that negative stuff out and just play." This sounds great, but they are leaving out one thing: how to do it.

Try this exercise. Pick out a sound or noise that is pretty constant in the room you are in right now. A fan, people talking, the radio, any sound will do. Focus on that sound for a moment. Now block it out. Don't listen to it, don't hear the sound, pretend it isn't there. Hey, we said block that sound out! You're still listening to it.

Being told to block something out is like being told to go pole vault. You may have a basic idea of what to do but no real knowledge of how to do it. Without learning how to do it, there is little chance for success.

A distraction is blocked out indirectly by focusing so intently on something else that the distraction is pushed out of your awareness. The key is to figure out what you should pay attention to and get really good at focusing on it.

By filling your mind with visualizations of what you want to do on this next pitch, all other distractions, such as an umpire's bad call, a fan or the other team yelling at you, the mechanical change your coach is trying to get you to make, the fact that you are the leadoff hitter in the next inning or that you are 0-for-your-last-8 at bats, are "blocked out."

Visualization will be discussed throughout the book (for more details, see the Appendix), but for now it's important to realize that you might not see the image clearly. It may be more of a feeling. You might hear the play happen in your head. Visualization is a skill. Like any other skill, it's developed with practice, so keep working with it.

In summary, once you have yourself under control, decide on a clear and simple plan for what you are going to do on the next pitch. Commit to that plan and get focused by seeing yourself do it (all of which is done in a matter of seconds). Now you're ready for the last step.

Step 3: Trust

> The goal of the mental game is to get to confidence. When you are confident, you trust yourself and let yourself perform. Instead of trying hard or pressing, it seems like you're on automatic pilot.

You've worked hard and paid your dues. Now relax and enjoy the fruits of that labor.

Making the Shift from "Thinking" to "Trusting"

When they're at their best, most players say their minds are clear. "I wasn't really thinking of anything," they might say. "I was just doing." When you find that groove, stay in it. There's no need to slow down when you have a green light.

Thinking too much is a big problem for players. Worrying about getting a hit or needing a pitching victory gets in the way of the spontaneous reactions that allow them to play their best.

Shifting from deciding on your plan between pitches to a trusting or "not thinking" mind-set allows you to play well during each pitch. The following suggestions can help you make the shift from thinking to trusting.

Self-Control

TRUST

Plan

1) The Breath

The breath often is effective in getting into your trusting mind-set. When you "think too much" your focus is inside on what you are thinking. When a pitch is thrown, regardless of whether you are throwing it, trying to hit it, preparing to catch it or looking to advance to the next base, you need to focus on the target. A good breath helps you do this. As you exhale, send your focus toward your target like a spotlight sending out a narrow beam of light.

2) Visualization

Seeing between pitches what you want to do helps your concentration and clicks you in to a trusting mind-set. Focus on the image of the ball being hit to you, your pitch hitting its target or a line drive whistling past the pitcher's ear to "block out" unwanted thoughts. The process of playing each pitch simply becomes: **SEE IT, DO IT.**

3) Cue Words

Although the goal is to think about nothing, realistically that doesn't happen too often. In fact, you probably have more "chatter" going on in your head than you hear on Little League infields.

> The closest thing to nothing is one. Remember this when you find yourself thinking too much. Instead of random thoughts, choose one word or a short phrase that directs your focus and instructs your actions. Say the word or words to yourself just before a pitch is thrown.

Mike Schmidt, former Philadelphia Phillies third baseman and 1995 inductee in baseball's Hall of Fame, calls this the "last conscious thought." It's your "theme" for the pitch or the at bat. From 1985 to 1989, Schmidt's "last conscious thought" as the pitcher entered his windup was "swing down and up the middle" and he would visualize hitting a line drive at the pitcher's knees. As his 548 career home runs attest, the ball often ended up out of the park instead, but those came by accident — he was programming himself to hit the ball up the middle.

Some of the thoughts he used at other times included "line drive to right-center," "keep the head down," "quick hands," "stay on top," and "(Roberto) Clemente," one of his role models.

Effective "cue words" capture what you are trying to accomplish and help you stay focused. What word or phrase would you say describes what you are doing when you are at your best?

Repeating these words before each pitch will help you shift from thinking to trusting and give you a chance to get to where you want to be — not thinking. It's easier for one thought to fade into no thoughts than for many random thoughts to disappear! (See the Appendix for more on self-talk.)

4) Performance-Related Triggers

Finally, use objects or pieces of equipment to trigger your focus. Pitchers can use the rubber as a "trigger" to shift into a trusting mind-set. Stepping on the rubber means you are ready for this pitch. Your focus is right here, right now. Don't step onto the rubber until you have a green light.

Hitters can use the batter's box in the same way. When you step into the box you're ready. Your focus is on the pitcher and the baseball. If you have a yellow or red light, take as much time as you need or are allowed. When you step in the box you are focused and ready for this pitch.

An imaginary "circle of focus" is helpful for fielders. As the pitcher is about to begin his delivery, take two steps forward into your "circle of focus." In that circle you are ready to focus on the baseball or the area over home plate from where the ball may come to you. If the ball isn't hit, step back, relax and repeat the process on the next pitch. Try pounding your glove once or twice in the circle to trigger your focus on the plate.

> The key is doing something that puts your focus outside of you. When you play well you trust your ability. Your focus isn't on you or your mechanics but on the ball or your target.

Trust What You've Got

Nobody feels 100 percent all the time. That's one of baseball's major challenges. Even if you recognize your yellow and red lights, even if you master the skills you need to get yourself under control, even if you have a clear and simple plan for each pitch and are committed to that plan, you won't feel totally confident every time you play.

> You've got to **TRUST WHAT YOU'VE GOT** and focus on what's working for you because that's what you can control. Instead of focusing on what's not working, focus on what is. Maybe you feel tired, your mechanics feel uncomfortable or your hands seem slow and you feel you're only at about 70 percent. Focus on the 70 percent you **do** have, not on the 30 percent you don't.

That's where the heads-up player puts his focus. He trusts that 70 percent. He focuses on what he can control and goes out and does battle with the weapons he has that day.

Don't give your opponent more credit than he's due. What makes you think **HE** has all his stuff together? Often, the pitcher thinks the hitter has his act together while the hitter thinks the pitcher has his act together. In reality, it's likely neither does! The player who knows what he does have and does the most with it is the one who wins the battle. You can't control what you don't have. Focus on what you can control. Focus on what you've got and trust it.

Exercise: Reasons to Trust

Your ability to trust yourself is largely determined by the strength of your conviction that you have clear reasons to trust yourself. What reasons do you have to trust yourself?

To solidify your confidence, make a list of your reasons to believe in yourself, reasons to support the belief that you are a mentally tough player. Confidence-enhancing thoughts will offset doubts that eventually creep into your mind. List your "reasons to trust" and keep them in a place where you will see them every day.

Use the space below to make your list. Examples include your hard work, past great performances, words of encouragement from someone you respect or your work on the mental game. Be clear, specific and detailed. There's strength in both clarity and numbers.

MY REASONS TO TRUST MYSELF:

_____

_____

_____

_____

_____

_____

_____

_____

_____

_____

_____

_____

_____

Putting It All Together: Examples of Players Playing One Pitch at a Time

Although the basic model of self-control, plan, trust holds true for each player and each part of the game, everyone has his own way of working through it. Your way of working through the process becomes your prepitch "routine." Your routine becomes what you are doing on the field. It's the way you play the game one pitch at a time.

A simple routine is recommended. Find an idea or two you like and work them into your game. You'll notice in these examples that the ideas we've talked about can be combined and used in many ways.

These are only examples of how the ideas presented could be applied. Use them in any way you find helpful.

Example 1: Infielder who is playing well

After a pitch is taken by the batter:

Self-control: Checks in, determines he's feeling confident and controlled (green light). **Plan:** "React to the ball." Visualizes a ground ball or two coming to him, makes the throw to first. **Trust:** The pitcher begins his motion, steps forward into his "circle of focus" and thinks, "Hit it to me."

Again the batter doesn't swing, the fielder steps out of his circle and relaxes before repeating the cycle on the next pitch.

Example 2: Infielder who just made an error

Remember Jim, the first baseman who let the ball go through his legs at the start of Chapter 3? Here's how he could have responded in an effort to get back to playing the game one pitch at a time.

> *"If you play the game like that — one pitch, one hitter, one inning at a time — the next thing you know you look up and you've won."*
> *— Rick Dempsey,*
> *major-league catcher*

After the ball gets in to second base and things settle down:

Self-control: Jim checks in, recognizes that he's tense, angry and has a million things running through his mind. This is at least a yellow if not a red light. To release the error, Jim turns around, takes his glove off and takes a good breath. After a few moments he lifts his head and chest (both of which had been hanging pretty low) and says to himself, "That one's over, get this next one." When he puts his glove back on and turns around he's ready to focus on the next pitch. **Plan:** "Two outs," he thinks. "Stay down on the ball." He visualizes the next batter hitting him the same ground ball. This time he stays down and makes the play. **Trust:** He takes another deep breath as he settles into his position holding the runner on first, his focus is on the pitcher. The batter takes the next pitch. Jim is still thinking about his error. He recognizes that as a yellow light and that he needs to use his routine again to focus on the next pitch.

Example 3: Pitcher throwing well

The following is an example of a pitcher whose routine is helping him maintain a fluid, positive rhythm. Let's say this is George, the pitcher throwing at the start of this chapter, facing one of the first two batters of the game.

As he gets the ball back from the catcher:

Self-control: He can feel he's in a good rhythm and that things are going well. That's a green light. **Plan:** He steps on the rubber (which means he's ready to go on this pitch), and takes a deep breath. He gets the sign from the catcher: curveball, down and in. He commits to throwing a curveball, down and in. **Trust:** He sends his focus out to his target, the catcher's mitt, and throws the pitch.

Example 4: Same pitcher after giving up a home run

George might have chosen to respond to the home run he gave up to the third hitter in the following way.

As he gets the new ball from the umpire:

Self-control: George recognizes that he's upset. He had a good inning going and all of the sudden he's behind 1-0. He wants to hurry and get back at the next guy. He's got at least a yellow, if not a red light. To get himself under control, George turns his back to home plate and walks to the area behind the mound. He looks out to his "focal point," the flag pole in center field, which reminds him that there's nothing he can do about the past or the future, and that he should relax and focus on this next pitch. He takes a good breath, turns around, and walks confidently back up on the mound. Before he steps on the rubber he pauses to make sure he's ready for the next pitch. **Plan:** He steps on the rubber and takes a deep breath. He then gets the sign from the catcher: fastball, low and away. He then commits to throwing a fastball, low and away. **Trust:** He directs his focus to his target, the catcher's mitt, and throws the pitch.

Example 5: Hitter who feels good at the plate

Just outside of the batter's box:

Self-control: He checks in and recognizes he feels good and he's confident he's going to drive the ball. That's a green light. **Plan:** He gets his signals from the third base coach. Nothing is on, so he's swinging away. "See the ball, hit the ball," he says to himself. **Trust:** He plants his back foot in the box, takes a good breath, and as he puts his front foot in the box he sends his focus to the pitcher and the baseball.

Example 6: Hitter who swings and misses at a curveball in the dirt

Let's say the same hitter takes a wild swing at a pitch well out of the strike zone. He steps out of the box and curses himself.

Self-Control: He recognizes he's not in control of himself. He was so anxious to get a hit that he didn't relax and give himself a chance to see the baseball. He bends over and picks up some dirt, squeezes it momentarily to put that last swing into it. He tosses the dirt behind him, throwing that last swing away with it. Next, he takes a deep breath to help get him regain control. **Plan:** He gets his signals from the third base coach. Nothing is on, so he's swinging away. "See the ball, hit the ball," he says to himself. **Trust:** He plants his back foot in the box, takes a good breath, and as he puts his front foot in the box he sends his focus to the pitcher and the baseball.

These are a few examples of how to play the game one pitch at a time. The skills discussed in this chapter are critical to playing with confidence, composure and consistency because it's what you do between pitches that determines what you do during the pitches. These strategies don't guarantee success, but they give you a routine that will help give you your best chance of being successful.

The Coach's Box

Coach, if you want your players to play the game one pitch at a time, reinforce the self-control, plan, trust process by using it to evaluate their performances. Ask your players, "Were you in control of yourself before each pitch?" "What was your plan on that pitch?" and "How well would you say you trusted yourself that time?"

Talk to them about their signal lights. Ask them where their yellow lights were today or if throwing a helmet meant a red light. When a player swings at a bad pitch, makes an error or has to deal with an obvious bad call by the umpire, ask him how he released it or what he did to release it and focus in on the next pitch. Using this terminology gives you a "language" to communicate with your players about the mental game.

Making Pregame Mental Preparation Routine

5

A primary goal of the mental game is to play with confidence. Believing you will succeed is the most important factor in determining how well you perform. Preparation is one of the most powerful means of gaining confidence: the more prepared you feel, the more confident you feel. This is true for a student about to take an exam, a surgeon faced with saving his patient's life or a batter stepping into the box to face a pitcher.

> Mental preparation is important to playing heads-up baseball because it's a source of confidence you can control. Getting hits, winning games and receiving praise from the coach build confidence, but they are all outside your circle of control. Don't base your confidence solely on things beyond your control. Build your confidence through solid mental preparation — something you can choose to do if you take responsibility for it.

The goal of mental preparation is to put you into a mind-set that enables you to play your best baseball. If you're like most players, this mind-set will be a combination of feeling pumped up, relaxed, focused, confident, loose and excited. It's a feeling of being centered and balanced. The goal is to get you to a green light which means you're under control. Having a green light before a game is important since you must have control of yourself before you can control your performance.

> *"The most important thing is how a guy prepares himself to do battle."*
> **— Hank Aaron, 6,856 career total bases**

Mental preparation also makes you more consistent. "One day I'll play great and the next I'll be brutal," some players complain. "What can I do to make myself a more consistent player?"

To be a more consistent player, be more consistent about the way you prepare for games. Be smarter and more disciplined in your thoughts and actions before the game. In this chapter, you will see how mental preparation techniques used by some of the game's steadiest players can be incorporated into your game.

A key in preparing for your next game begins as soon as your last game or practice ends. Heads-up players learn as much as they can each day. An effective teacher reviews the main points of the day's lesson at the end of a class period. It's to your benefit to take some time after each performance to draw as much useful information as you can from what you did. The chapter will conclude with some thoughts on how to constructively evaluate games and practices.

Preparation for Greatness: *A Talk with Hank Aaron*

Hank Aaron, who overcame enormous pressure (including threats to his life) to break Babe Ruth's career home run record, was amazingly consistent over the course of his 23-year major-league career. An average year consisted of a .305 batting average, 100 RBIs and 32 home runs! Also mind-boggling is the fact that Aaron is the career total base leader, and if you measured the number of bases he is ahead of the man in second place on that list, Stan Musial, his lead is a distance of more than 12 miles!

How did he do it? Physical talent helped, but those kinds of numbers go way beyond physical talent. In an interview, Aaron discusses the keys to his success. Although he's talking about hitting, the same ideas work for pitching and fielding.

Aaron: *Well the first thing that comes to mind when you start talking about the mental aspects of hitting is how a guy usually prepares himself to do battle, to go out and face the pitcher. I think so many hitters don't know mentally how to get themselves prepared to play or to hit against a pitcher. Every pitcher pitches differently, and you have to approach it that way.*

You have to study the pitcher. If you're hitting against Sandy Koufax, his fastball is not like Bob Gibson's fastball. And Gibson's fastball is certainly not the same as a Don Drysdale fastball, and Tom Seaver's is different from all of them.

Question: What goes into preparing yourself mentally?

Aaron: *You visualize it. You see it in your head, you think about it and you understand that no matter who you're facing or who you faced the day before, it's not the same. Every pitcher is different.*

Question: So from a preparation standpoint, how would a day go? Let's say you're going to play the Mets and Jerry Koosman is going to pitch.

Aaron: *Well, mentally, my whole pattern of thinking would be "What is it that I need to focus in on, that I need to think about as a hitter? What does Koosman do well and how is he going to try to get me out in different situations?" Then I would start visualizing — like I'm standing at the plate with, say, runners at first and second, or second and third — how he's going to pitch me in that given situation. Then I would start visualizing, for example, if the bases were loaded, how he would try to get me out.*

I would then look at it in the sixth inning, seventh inning, eighth inning, and so on, and I would put myself in all of these different positions and put him in the same positions and try to figure out what is best

Hank Aaron hits his 710th home run. Mental preparation was the key to his ability to focus at the plate. (National Baseball Library and Archive, Cooperstown, N.Y.)

for him and what I am going to be looking for. So, I visualized all these different situations.

Question: You mentioned coming to the park and "focusing." What does that mean to you?

Aaron: *That means tuning out everything else. You get to the ballpark sometimes and you see three or four guys sitting around the corner playing cards, you see somebody over in the corner talking on the telephone — anything other than taking the time out to focus in on what they have to do. When you get to the ballpark, you ought to be able to get yourself in tune to knowing who the pitcher is that you're going to face. It's kind of like taking a harness and putting it on a horse and letting him look nowhere but straight ahead. If you concentrate, and start thinking about what you're doing, consistently, you're going to automatically become a better hitter. That's what separates the guy that's going to hit .300 from the guy that's going to hit .270.*

And you know what this does for you? All these things are working together, so you don't have to have somebody behind you telling you to keep your eye on the ball. You're automatically going to do that. That's what hitting instructors tell you all the time: "Watch the ball, watch the ball." Well, hell, I know that. But if you don't watch it, you're not going to hit it. All of that comes from the same thing that we're talking about, concentration. Visualizing what you've got to do. And if you can do all these things, you're going to be a better hitter.

Question: You were amazingly consistent over an incredible number of years. To what would you attribute that?

Aaron: *The same thing that we're talking about. I think my ability to focus was a lot different than the average guy's. A lot of guys would be distracted by different things. I was totally in tune with what I was doing. I was involved with a lot of things — I went through divorce, I went through a having a child die, I went through the home run record — but as soon as I got to the ballpark my focus would always change. A lot of people used to carry things on the field, but for some reason, once I put that uniform on, or once I walked into that clubhouse, no matter what happened at home, I could totally get focused. I could focus in on pitchers and what I had to do.*

Hank Aaron developed a routine before each game and at bat of visualizing pitches that might be thrown to him in different game situations. He credits this routine for his consistency and ability to handle pressure. Repeated visualization allowed him to focus on nothing but each pitch when he was at the plate.

In our terms, his focus on the ingredients of hitting — especially seeing the baseball and trying to hit it — pushed aside all distractions, including death threats, during the home run chase. He cleared any obstacles he might have put in his path by focusing solely on the pitcher and the baseball.

Taking Responsibility for Your Preparation

What thoughts and actions lead to your best performances? What do you do and think before your best games? Visualizing himself facing that night's pitcher helped Hank Aaron focus and put him in the mind-set needed to play his best. You need to discover what works best for you.

Only you are responsible for your mental preparation. Nobody can do it for you. It's great when coaches, teammates or friends do things that help get you up for games, or when you get motivated by having a beautiful field, nice weather or an opponent that you always do well against to get you going. But don't count on things like that to help get you mentally prepared because they are outside of your control. **Players who rely on factors outside of their control for their mental preparation are inconsistent players.**

The goal is to build a predetermined series of actions called a routine that you can use to consistently get yourself focused and into a mind-set to play your best baseball. A well thought out routine takes the randomness out of your preparation and helps you **choose** effective things to do and think before each performance, rather than leaving these important elements to chance. Developing a routine means you have taken responsibility for your mental preparation.

A routine is like a funnel that channels your thoughts and actions before a game, at bat or pitch to where they need to be. It sets conditions that give you the best chance of having a peak performance. Instead of waiting around for your confident, focused mind-set to happen, you proactively take the physical and mental actions that have led to your best performances in the past. If you don't go through the process of (1) determining what you need to do to prepare and then (2) doing those things before each game, you are leaving your performance to chance. Some days "it" will be there and some days it won't.

> "If you fail to prepare, be prepared to fail."
> — Anonymous

Think of your routine as a checklist of things to do before you perform. Pilots use a checklist before taking off to ensure a safe flight. The checklist is the result of what technicians and pilots have learned about safe flights in the past. Your preperformance routine is a checklist of things to do before you perform, a list of things that have led to your best performances in the past.

A routine is not a superstition. A routine prepares you by focusing your energies on things you can control, whereas superstitions and rituals are appeals to some supernatural power. If you feel a superstition helps you, use it. But we prefer you focus on things you can control.

A pregame routine won't guarantee that you are totally confident, totally focused, and in the zone for each game. But it will consistently give you your best chance of being at your best which is what the mental game is all about.

The section below has several ideas to help you mentally prepare for a baseball game or practice. Choose the ones you like best and see yourself using on a consistent basis. The written exercise at the end of the chapter is an opportunity to think through the thoughts and actions that lead to **YOUR** best performances and help you develop a routine you can use before each game.

Before Going to the Ballpark

Make it a habit to get plenty of sleep, eat well and do things your mother would tell you to do. Young players have bodies that seem to keep going regardless of whether they get "enough" sleep or eat "right" every day. As a result, it's not unusual for players to treat their gloves better than their own bodies. Every doctor, trainer, coach and mom in the world knows your body performs better when it has quality fuel to run on. Instead of burgers and fries, mix in a salad or some other vegetable as part of your pregame routine.

1) Give yourself a steady diet of positive thoughts. Just as you will play better if you fill your body with fruits and vegetables, you will also play better if you consistently feed yourself positive thoughts about the game. Negative thinking is junk food for the mind. You wouldn't pound down a couple of Twinkies on your way out to the mound or your defensive position, so don't make yourself sick with negative thoughts. Like junk food, negative thinking not only hurts the way you feel at the moment, it also builds up over time and weighs you down.

When you think about baseball, think about playing well. See yourself hitting line drives up the middle, throwing great pitches and making solid defensive plays. Tune in to what you are telling yourself and make sure it is healthy, confidence-building stuff and not junk food.

Thinking confidence-enhancing thoughts is easy when you play well. Heads-up players are able to do it when things aren't going so well and when they aren't getting the "outcomes" they want.

If you sit around all day and think about playing badly, expect to go to the park and play badly. If you spend your time thinking about playing great, you go to the park expecting to play great.

It's not recommended that you spend all day thinking about the game. That would probably burn you out. But when you find yourself thinking about the upcoming game **BE AWARE OF WHAT YOU ARE THINKING.** A good way to check in on your thinking is to ask yourself, "Am I looking forward to playing?" "Looking forward" is positive mental preparation. If you dread going to the ballpark, that's a yellow light at the least! Take a breath and get those thoughts turned around.

Here's a suggestion: set aside 10 minutes or so during the day when you are going to think about the game. Go over what you want to have happen during the game (accomplishing your mission, for example) and review your "reasons to trust" from Chapter 1. Having done your mental preparation, you are free to study, have fun or spend some quality time with your family and friends without worrying about the game.

2) Do some relaxation and imagery. Thousands of athletes in virtually all sports have found relaxation and imagery sessions to be a helpful way of preparing for competition. Relaxation and imagery is discussed in detail and a sample script is presented in the appendix at the end of the book. Basically it involves finding a quiet environment and going through a simple series of steps that help you get totally relaxed. Then, like Aaron, visualize yourself performing successfully in different situations. The result is greater self-control, a clearer vision of what you want to do during the game and a stronger sense of confidence. (This could be your "10 minutes or so" we mentioned in the last paragraph.)

> *"If your stomach disputes you, lie down and pacify it with cool thoughts."*
> **— Satchel Paige,**
> **from How to Stay Young**

At the Ballpark

1) Choose a time or action that signifies leaving all other roles behind to become a baseball player. Hank Aaron said that once he got to the ballpark he left his other concerns aside to focus only on baseball.

> It's very important for players to pick definite times when they say "OK, now I'm a baseball player; all my other concerns can wait until I'm done playing or practicing." This doesn't mean that you can't talk casually about school, movies or whatever, but don't talk about them for long and never lose sight of your mission as a ballplayer.

Changing into your uniform is a great way to symbolize a change in who you are. As you take off your normal clothes, say to yourself that you are taking off all of your concerns and problems not related to baseball. Hang those problems in your locker and leave them there. They will be there when you put them back on after the game.

When you put on your uniform, tell yourself you are putting on the ultimate baseball player. The uniform is a reminder you are prepared, confident, focused and ready to do battle.

Other options for the time you "become a ballplayer" include when you leave your house or apartment, enter the ballpark or walk into the clubhouse. You could also say that when you get out of your car in the ballpark lot you "park" all of your concerns there.

2) Familiarize yourself with your environment. As soon as possible, go to the mound, the batter's box or your defensive position — any place you are going to or might be performing during the game. Check the view, the grass and the dirt; get a feel for the area. Pitchers should stand on the mound as soon as they have a chance. Whether a starter or a possible reliever, check the way the plate and the rest of the field look. "Make friends" with the mound before the game so you are prepared when you come into the game.

Hitters need to check the view from home plate before the game to feel more comfortable with the way things look during that first at bat — especially if you don't take batting practice from home plate before the game. This is especially important at another team's park, but it's not a bad idea when you're at home.

3) Choose your focal point. Part of familiarizing yourself with the field is picking your focal point. A focal point is an object, usually somewhere in or beyond the outfield, at which you can look when you have a yellow or red light and need to get back under control. Before the game begins, find your focal point and review in your mind what it "says" to you. Pick something you know will be there during the game. A car parked behind the left field fence isn't a good choice because it might be gone when you need it!

4) Set your mission(s). This is a big one. Any time before a game is a good time to clarify your mission or missions for the day. You may have a mission for batting practice and another for the game (see Chapter 2 to review this idea). Well before the game begins, repeat your mission to yourself and visualize yourself successfully completing it. Your mission provides intensity and purpose to your actions, and helps keep you from simply "going through the motions." Whatever you want your career to be like, be like that today.

The Team Stretch

1) Check in on how you're feeling. Often you are rushed or distracted during the time leading up to the team stretch, so stretching is a good opportunity for you to tune in to your mental state and see how your body feels. The chattering and razzing that usually go on at this time are fun and help keep you loose, but discipline yourself for at least a few moments to focus on some mental preparation.

For example, ask yourself: am I where I want to be mentally right now? Am I excited for the game? Am I too excited? Too relaxed? Is my head in the ballpark or am I thinking about concerns I have outside of baseball? If you're where you want to be, look for your green light and go with it. If you need to make an adjustment, now is the time to make it. Use tools such as imagery, the breath, self-talk, extra stretching and extra physical work to raise, lower or otherwise adjust yourself. If you wait until the first pitch is thrown it will probably be too late.

2) Use your breath while stretching. A slow, steady breath gets you into the present moment, helps you check in on yourself and enhances the quality of your stretches.

Pregame Batting Practice and Infield/Outfield

Do what you are going to do in the game. It's easy to go through the motions of getting loose, taking batting practice, taking pregame infield and starting the game without really getting prepared. Just because you "put in your time" on the field prior to a game doesn't mean you're prepared to play at your best. The pregame process can become so monotonous that even if you do prepare yourself physically you don't come close to preparing yourself mentally. You can be physically present in pregame workouts without being present mentally. Your challenge before each game is to prepare with purpose and intent. Your challenge is to prepare as if you are on a mission.

BP should stand for Baseball Practice, not just batting practice. BP is a time to work on what you are going to be doing in a game. If you are going to try to hit the ball up the middle during a game, try to do it in BP. If you are going to play defense with intensity and focus during the game, do it in BP. If you're going to run bases aggressively during the game, do the

> *"I tried to practice the way I played . . . You can't practice one way and then expect to do it differently in a game."*
> *— Hall of Famer Al Kaline*

same thing in BP. We'll talk more in Chapter 9 about working on your mental game during practice, but here are a few things to do:

- Be mentally prepared to hit before you step into the cage, don't get into the cage to get ready to hit. In other words, prepare to hit, don't hit to prepare.
- Take a breath before each pitch.
- Pitchers, if you were going to start the biggest game of your career

later this week, what would you do today during your time at the park to prepare?
• Check in regularly to determine if you are focused or just going through the motions.

You don't need to go 100 percent for the full practice. Take a few breaks when you are in the field. The goal is quality practice, not quantity practice.

Exercise: **What Do You Need to Do to Prepare?**

You now have quite a bit of information about preparing to play a game. The goal in this last section is to help you pull some of these ideas together (along with other ideas you've found helpful) into a concrete strategy, a routine you can follow as you prepare for a game.

Your routine funnels your thoughts and feelings to the way you want to be thinking and feeling before a game. Whether you are playing well, in a slump or nervous about the upcoming game, you go to your routine to give yourself your best chance of success. The more thought and writing you put into these exercises, the more you get out of them.

> • **How did you prepare for your best performances? What did you do, think and feel during your pregame preparation?**
>
>
>
> • **List what you want to do mentally before each game (i.e., visualize yourself playing, remind yourself of any mechanical cues you want to keep in mind, positive statements you want to make to yourself, how you want to carry your body). Be specific.**

It's often helpful to tie together mental and physical aspects of your preparation. You and your team already have some sort of physical routine you go through before each game. The mental aspects we have been discussing are easily integrated into your physical routine. Improving your mental preparation doesn't involve doing a lot of new things, but it does involve doing the things you do differently — with a purpose in mind. Using the information in this chapter and your answers to the last two questions as a guide, write in the funnel what you do mentally at each of the following times:

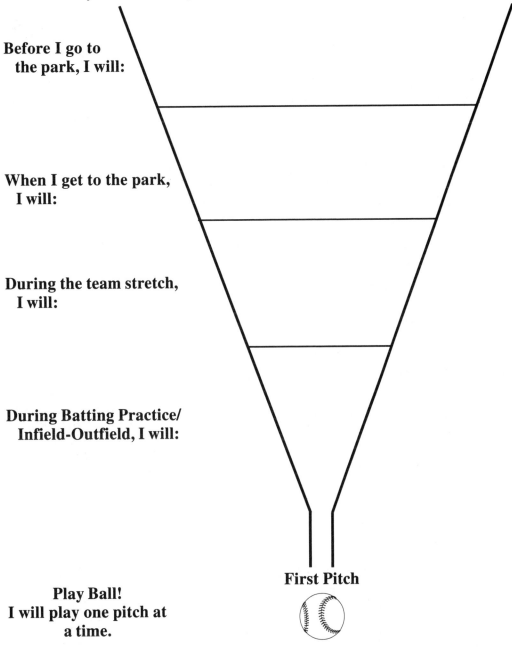

**Before I go to
the park, I will:**

**When I get to the park,
I will:**

**During the team stretch,
I will:**

**During Batting Practice/
Infield-Outfield, I will:**

First Pitch

**Play Ball!
I will play one pitch at
a time.**

Like an airplane pilot, make what you wrote a "checklist" of things to do before you "take off" into a game. This is only a starting place, however. It's important to consistently evaluate how effective your routine is at getting you ready to play. **There undoubtedly will be changes you'll want to make as you gain experience using your routine**. Maintaining an awareness of what works for you and what doesn't is vital to becoming the most consistent and mentally tough player you can be.

Postgame Learning

One of your primary objectives as a ballplayer is to learn as much as you can. The more you learn about yourself and about the game, the better player you'll be and the more fun you'll have. Players often fail to take advantage of the time they have after a game to review a performance. Analyzing what you did right helps solidify your confidence; analyzing what went wrong helps you catch and correct your mistakes. The more quickly you catch mistakes, the less likely you are to fall into a prolonged slump.

An example of making effective use of this idea comes from one major-league player who would replay his four at bats in his head when he got back home or to his hotel. He would image four more at bats with the feeling and results he wanted before he went to bed at night. Thus, he took four at bats and turned them into 12.

Listed below are questions you can ask yourself after a game. Use them any way you want: you might want to answer all or them or pick a small number of them. Write your answers in a journal or take a few minutes and think them through in your head.

Personal Feedback Sheet
(Answer all or select a few questions each time)

- What was today's mission(s)? Were you successful in accomplishing it/them?

- Did you use a pregame routine? How did it work? Are there any changes you want to make in that routine that could make it more helpful?

- What grade would you give yourself on the quality of your pregame preparation?

- How was your confidence today? What helped and what hurt your confidence?

- Did you play the game one pitch at a time?

- Were you in **control** of yourself before each pitch?

- Did you have a **plan** for what you wanted to do on each pitch?

- Did you **trust** yourself on each pitch?

- What yellow and red lights did you experience today? In other words, what upset you or got you out of your rhythm before or during the game?

- How did you experience those yellow and red lights? (Where did you get tense? Did the game speed up? What were your thoughts at the time?, etc.)

- What did you do (what tools did you use) to try to get yourself back under control? How effective were you at getting yourself back?

- How well were you focused on the **PROCESS** of playing the game instead of the **OUTCOME** of your actions?

Check back on what you said was your mission for your career in baseball. Is how you went about your business today consistent with that mission? Examples might include: Are you proud of what you did today? Did you respect the game of baseball today? Did you get the most out of your ability? Did you learn? Did you have fun?

The Coach's Box

Coaches, help your players develop the habit of constructively evaluating their performances by periodically having them fill out "feedback sheets" that you make up using the questions provided and others of your own. In addition to giving you some insights into your players, the questions make them think about the mental game and tell them that you think it is important.

Changing the questions on the sheets and only having them filled out occasionally will help keep the sheets meaningful for the players.

Pitching:
Trust Your Stuff

At this point we have covered the basic ideas and tools of playing heads-up baseball and discussed how they apply to all phases of the game. The next three chapters will focus on key mental concerns specific to pitching, hitting, fielding and baserunning.

> In no part of the game is being heads-up and playing the game one pitch at a time more crucial than on the mound. Pitching is the most important part of the game. The confidence a pitcher has in his next pitch is probably the most important variable in baseball. This chapter is designed to enhance your ability to believe in each pitch you throw.

The Mission

The place to begin a discussion of the mental aspects of pitching is with your mission. Why do you pitch? What do you enjoy or love about pitching? Where does pride show up in your pitching? Putting answers to these questions in the front of your mind will make the rest of the mental game, and therefore the game as a whole, come much easier.

If you pitch because you think it's fun, for example, have fun doing it. If you pitch because you love it, love it while you're doing it. If you practice this approach, the chances of stressing out or choking during the game are greatly reduced.

Exercise: **Pitcher, Know Yourself**

A big part of successful pitching is knowing yourself. You often hear coaches tell players to "stay within yourself." Everyone agrees that it's important, but what does it mean?

Staying within yourself means doing what you are capable of doing and not trying to do "too much." The key to staying "within yourself" is to know your capabilities, your strengths and weaknesses, and what type of pitcher you are. Only then are you in a position to know if you are "within yourself."

Get to know yourself a little better by spending a few minutes responding to the following questions:

1) **What are your strengths and weaknesses as a pitcher?**

2) **What is your best pitch?**

3) **How do you get most of your outs? (Review any pitching charts you may have for this one; you may not realize how most of the hitters you face are retired.)**

4) **Complete the following statement at least three different ways: "I am most effective when:"**

5) **When you are pitching well, what are you focused on during your delivery? (the glove, a spot on the glove, a spot on the catcher, etc.)**

6) **When you are pitching well, what is your mind-set or attitude? (examples might include: "Here it is, try to hit it," "You can't hit me," "I'm in control," etc.)**

7) **List the events that can happen during a game that can throw you off your rhythm (i.e.; walking a batter, giving up a home run, an error behind you).**

Three Common Yellow or Red Light Problems

A big part of knowing yourself is knowing how you respond under pressure. Although each pitcher's response to adversity is unique, three mental mistakes or pitching patterns are seen quite regularly — **Prayer Pitching, Primal Pitching** and **Perfect Pitching.** All result from a lack of trust. It's important to recognize these patterns so you can get yourself out of them as quickly as possible.

The first is a shift from a mind-set that says, "The ball is going right there" (to your target) or, "I'm in control of this game," to a mind-set that says, "I hope he doesn't hit this pitch too hard." As a result of this shift, the pitcher often loses his mechanics, his velocity and, finally, the game. Throwing a pitch with "hope" is called "Prayer Pitching." It's rarely effective. The baseball gods tend to reward those who take charge of their performances more than those who look for outside intervention! Remember, a pitch thrown with conviction and commitment is much more effective than one launched with a hope and a prayer behind it.

Another common response to adversity is forgetting the concept of "pitching" and reverting to simply "throwing." The pitcher in trouble often tries to get out of the jam by throwing harder. Since he missed the strike zone with one pitch, he tries to throw the next one HARDER, following that one with an even HARDER delivery, and so on. This progression, or, more accurately, regression, is so naturally human, in fact, that it seems to have its roots in the days of the cave man. Thus, we call it "Primal Pitching."

Pitchers spiraling out of control often fall into "Primal Pitching."

Ironically, Primal Pitching's actual effect is opposite of what a pitcher intends. The effort to throw the ball harder produces tension that reduces the efficiency of his motion which actually slows the ball down. Since the primal pitcher tends to rush his body through his motion, his pitches are typically high. Further, throwing "harder" tends to flatten most pitches, ironing out any running or sinking movement the ball might normally have. Straight fastballs at any speed will get hit hard sooner or later. Clearly, the Primal Pitcher is not in control of himself, his mechanics or the baseball.

The opposite of Primal Pitching is "Perfect Pitching." Rather than trying to throw harder, some pitchers respond to pressure by attempting to make perfect pitches. They nibble on the corners of the plate, or at least they try to. Since they are aiming for such a small target, they miss a lot which means a lot of walks, and all of a sudden the bases are loaded with nobody out. Unaware that it's his thinking that got him in trouble in the first place, the Perfect Pitcher thinks: "Now I **REALLY** need to be perfect!" Before long the manager has a perfect reason to change pitchers.

Perfect Pitching is common in players who have just moved to a higher level of the game. A high school pitcher making his first start, a college pitcher in his first year, and a professional who has just moved up a level tend to feel that, "In order to succeed here, I've got to take my pitching up a notch. In fact, I'll need to be perfect to get these guys out." They get away from the very stuff that got them the opportunity to advance in the first place.

> Primal Pitching and Perfect Pitching result from the false assumption that pitchers must strike batters out. That's not the case. Successful hitting takes timing; a successful pitcher throws off the batter's timing. Think of your job more as getting the batter to hit the ball poorly. If you are interested in throwing a lot of innings, you're much better using one, two or three pitches to get hitters to ground out than striking them out with six or seven. Besides, the more of your pitches a batter sees, the more comfortable he becomes with you. Also, if your fielders know the ball will be hit regularly, they become more alert.

Your job is to hit the mitt. The Chicago White Sox tell their pitchers that they are "professional glove hitters." They recognize that hitting the mitt is the only thing a pitcher can control, so their pitchers focus on that. As Angels pitcher Mark Langston puts it, "You have to realize that you aren't throwing to a batter, you're throwing to a catcher."

> "A pitcher should never 'throw' the ball; he should make a pitch. A pitch has a purpose and a target."
> — *Bert Blyleven*

You don't need to make great pitches to get guys out. Watch batting practice one time: the pitcher tries to let the batter hit the ball, but more often than not the batter doesn't hit the ball well or, if he does, it goes right to one of the fielders.

We aren't saying you should go out and throw batting practice during a game, but keep in mind that getting a hit is tough. If you walk guys and pitch from behind in the count, though, hitting becomes much easier. Pitch with the mind-set of wanting to make good pitches, not great ones. Be focused and confident when you pitch, and commit to the pitch you are about to throw.

> The bottom line to all three of these mental mistakes is trust. Free yourself up and trust that the ball is going to go where you want it to go. When you "try hard" or attempt to steer the ball to your target, you "short arm" the ball and don't follow through resulting is a loss of velocity and location on your pitches. This is what Marcel Lachemann was talking about in Chapter 3 — your mechanics fail because of your faulty thinking.

The phrase heard over and over is, "Throw the ball, don't aim it." That's just another way to say, "Trust yourself." Let it go. Have some fun. Love it. Free it up. Recall the time you felt the best on the mound, whether it was in a game or the bullpen, and you'll know what we mean.

Pregame Tour: Get to Know Your Workplace

One of your first tasks after arriving at the field is to **familiarize yourself with your environment.** Go to the mound the first chance you get, especially on the road. Stand on the mound and study the view you will have during the game. Feel the dirt; feel the height and slope of the mound. Pick your focal point for the game and think of what that focal point will remind you of. This is where you will be working; don't wait until you come into the game to pitch to make your first visit. Familiarity breeds confidence.

If you find any imperfections on the mound, there's no sense in getting upset about them. Focus on what you can control. Rather than a "This mound stinks" mentality, ask yourself, "What do I need to do to pitch well on this mound?" **Spend your time solving the problem, not dwelling on it.**

This is also a good time to assign **special significance to objects on and around the mound.** For example, designate the mound as a place where only positive, productive thoughts and attitudes are allowed. If you feel negative stuff during the game, get off the mound; don't come back up until you're ready to have a positive focus on this next pitch. It's OK to get upset; you're not a robot. Just recognize when you are upset and get off the mound.

To give yourself a place to go to release your negative emotions, designate an area behind or to the side of the mound as your "toilet," a place to relieve yourself of the wasteful negative energy you are carrying in your head and body. Spend whatever time you need there and flush away your negatives. Then, go back to the mound feeling lighter and more positive!

Finally, treat the rubber with respect. Realize that it is the source of all action in the game. Don't set your foot on it until you are ready to throw the next pitch. **Think that the pitch starts when you put your foot on the rubber.** When you put your foot on the rubber, you are saying that you are ready for the next pitch. "Ready" means right here, right now, this pitch.

It's not uncommon to see a pitcher put his foot on the rubber while shaking his head in disgust or suddenly snapping it forward. When you see a player's head jerk like a chicken's does when it walks it's a sure sign he's swearing. If he's swearing, he's upset about the last pitch and still isn't focused totally on the next pitch — and probably won't be when he throws it.

One of a pitcher's advantages is controlling when the pitch starts. You run the show and everyone else reacts to you. Don't forget that. Not only is it a fact of the game, but it's an attitude the best pitchers take to the mound with them. Sure, batters can step out of the box and take their time getting ready, but nothing happens until you decide to throw the ball. Since you know that you control when a pitch is thrown, **never throw a pitch unless you are ready.** So, when you put your foot on the rubber, think, "This pitch."

The Bullpen

Once you are familiar with your environment, your pregame or pre-appearance routine revolves around a three-step progression:

1) Get your body ready to throw.
2) Get comfortable with your pitches.
3) Practice pitching.

Your first task is to get your body ready to throw. This will normally include some running, stretching and light throwing. Once your body is ready, turn your focus to your pitches. Throw your fastball until you start to feel comfortable with it; then move to your curveball, then your change-up, or whatever pitches you throw. Keep in mind your physical cues to throwing each pitch, and throw with the goal of getting a comfortable feel for each one.

When you are somewhat comfortable with your pitches, start throwing as you would during the game. You don't often throw the same pitch twice in a row during a game, and rarely would you throw the same pitch three consecutive times, so don't do it now. The way to get ready for a game is to go through your routine just as you would during a game: get under control, commit to the pitch and trust yourself on the pitch. Work imaginary hitters. Even better, have a teammate stand in the batter's box to provide a game-like simulation. How are you going to pitch the first three hitters? If you've already pitched to them in the bullpen it will be easier to get them out in the game.

It's important to remember that we are speaking at a general level about how to prepare to come into a game. Many, if not most, pitchers build a more specific routine around the basic idea of getting their bodies ready first, then focusing on their pitches, then getting their pitching ready. You may feel that you already do this, but being aware of the progression adds quality and purpose to your actions.

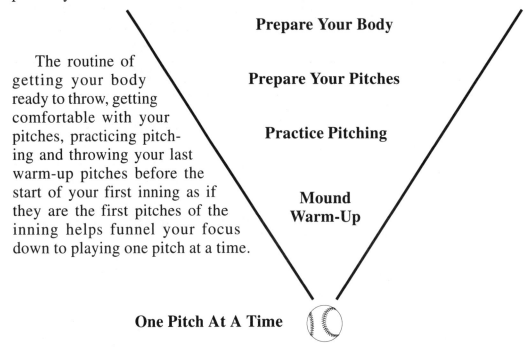

Prepare Your Body

The routine of getting your body ready to throw, getting comfortable with your pitches, practicing pitching and throwing your last warm-up pitches before the start of your first inning as if they are the first pitches of the inning helps funnel your focus down to playing one pitch at a time.

Prepare Your Pitches

Practice Pitching

Mound Warm-Up

One Pitch At A Time

Warm-Up Pitches on the Mound

Pitchers frequently fail to use their pitches before the start of an inning to their advantage. Don't look at them as simply a time to get loose; use them to click yourself in to what you are doing and what you want to do in the game. While you certainly need to get loose, throw your final pitches the way you will throw the ball once the inning begins.

Tell yourself that the inning begins with the first of your final three warm-up pitches. Take a good breath before each one and focus the same way you will when a batter stands in. Thus, when a hitter does step in, you're throwing your fourth pitch, not your first. Again, the basic principle is **practice what you are going to do in the game.**

Taking It from the Bullpen to the Game

"I'm fine in the bullpen, but when I get into the game it feels like I'm a different pitcher; everything seems to fall apart." This is one of the biggest problems for pitchers. It must be overcome to find out how good you can be as a pitcher.

You could say that everything we have talked about in this book could be used as a way to resolve this issue, but here are some specific ideas to help bring your bullpen stuff into the game with you.

> **Get into the right mind-set.** First, keeping a mind-set of having fun, loving what you are doing and generally keeping the game "in perspective" can be a big help. Those mind-sets clear the obstacles that lead to problems on the mound.

Similarly, a trusting mind-set also helps bring your bullpen stuff into the game with you. Pitching with trust is pitching with a sense of "freedom" — free from any worry, doubt, tension or fear. Many pitchers benefit by making their mission to throw "free and easy."

> *"You've got to trust yourself out there. Trust allows you to make the pitch that gets you the ground ball instead of the base hit."*
> — *Jim Abbott, New York Yankees*

Look at it this way: the worst that can happen to you in an outing has probably already happened once and you lived to tell the tale. You don't want the worst to happen, but knowing you can handle it frees you from having to worry about it. Go out and enjoy pitching whether that means focusing on having fun, getting intense or some other mind-set that leads to your best performances.

Project Confidence. As we (and Dennis Eckersley) spoke about earlier, it's important to carry yourself in a confident, even cocky, way. Not only do your teammates and opposition read your body language to see how good you feel about yourself, but holding your head up, shoulders back and chest out helps you feel more confident in yourself. The more confidence you have, the more likely you are to throw the ball to the best of your ability. **A key to playing heads-up baseball is to keep your head up!**

> **Trust What You Have.** Regardless of how well you carry yourself, you aren't going to have total confidence every time you pitch. Trust what you DO have. If you've got 80 percent of your stuff, for example, go out and do battle with that. Don't dwell on the 20 percent you don't have and don't give the hitter too much credit — he probably doesn't have all of his stuff together, either! A pitch thrown with trust and conviction is less likely to get hit hard than a pitch thrown with doubt or fear.

Put Quality in Your Bullpens. It's easier to get into a trusting mind-set when you feel you have good reason to trust yourself. Thus, the quality of your work in the bullpen during practice and the time before coming into the game is critical. In general, approach your bullpens with the sense of purpose and focus you will have in a game. Treat your bullpens with the respect you treat your throwing in a game. Simulate game conditions as best you can in the bullpen. Confidence comes with comfort, with familiarity and with experience. If you try to do something in a game that you haven't done in practice, don't be surprised if you don't feel confident!

Part of this quality practice is focusing on the process, on the ingredients of pitching. There are so many things beyond your control when you are pitching that you need to do a great job with what you can control if you want to consistently succeed. Your prepitch routine pulls the ingredients together and gives you something to go to when your good rhythm isn't there. **Be sure you are working with your routine in the bullpens.**

Enhance the quality of your bullpens by always having a mission in mind. Before you start, ask, "What am I trying to accomplish with this pen?" Are you going to focus on your breaking ball, your change up, your routine, on staying back, on releasing the ball out in front, on being "free and easy" or on establishing a good sense of rhythm? If you don't have a mission and just "go through the motions," your body may get the physical workout it needs, but you aren't learning or preparing the way you need to if you want to be at your best.

One mission that often is helpful for a pen is to come up with cue words or phrases that seem to be the keys for each pitch you throw. Paying attention might lead you to find, for example, that the key to your breaking ball right now is to "stay back," and the key to your fastball is to get "out in front." You then have those phrases handy and can incorporate them into your routine in your next outing if you have trouble with either of those pitches.

Focus on the Mitt. Another key to taking your bullpen stuff to the mound is focusing on your target. Don't focus on thoughts like "I don't feel right," "I don't have my good fastball," "I always have the worst luck when I'm out here," "This mound is a joke," or things of that nature. Get control of yourself, focus on your target and throw the ball.

Whether you are throwing to the catcher's mitt or to another spot on his body, your target is the final focus you'll have before you throw a pitch. As obvious as this sounds, pitchers, especially those who are struggling, often fail to focus on a target. They get caught up in trying to get the batter out or hoping the ball doesn't get hit too hard. Getting the batter out is not something you can control. While it certainly is a concern, you can't afford to have that be your focus.

Exactly what pitchers focus on varies from a tiny spot to a larger area. The answer to what you should focus on can be found in your best performances. Think back to what you were focusing on when you've been at your best. It's important to know what has worked best for you so you can choose that focus on each pitch.

You Don't Need Your Best Stuff. Another important thought to keep in mind is that you don't have to have your best stuff to get guys out. If you are like most pitchers, you get a lot of guys out on "bad" pitches. Can you recall striking a batter out or getting him to pop up on a pitch that wasn't anywhere near where you wanted it to go? (Remember that you can't control what a batter does, you can't make him swing or keep him from swinging.) At the same time you've probably had great stuff and gotten hit hard. That's just the way pitching is.

According to Bert Blyleven, "If you look at all the starts you are going to have in a season, 10 percent of the time you'll have great stuff, 10 percent of the time you'll have nothing and 80 percent of the time you'll have really average stuff." His comment is consistent with the thoughts of most pitchers we've talked to at all levels of baseball. Thus, the deciding factor on whether or not you have a good season is how mentally tough you are during that 80 percent.

Bert Blyleven found visualizing his pitch just before he threw it to be a key to succeeding on those days when he didn't have great stuff.

Given a choice, you'd like to have your best stuff all of the time, but in reality, most of the time you'll have pretty average stuff. Quality, season-long preparation will help you have "it" more often, but the kind of stuff you have on a given day is not totally under your control. The key to getting guys out is keeping your head together and not getting into Prayer, Primal or Perfect Pitching.

Approach Success. The key to pitching is in your approach, regardless of what kind of stuff you have. Your approach is the only thing you can control and the only thing you can keep constant in the unpredictable world of pitching. Maintaining a solid approach gives you your best chance of being successful.

Therefore, don't fall into the trap that what you do in the bullpen is going to be what you do in the game. If you have a great bullpen, great, but when you get to the mound you'd better respect the game (don't take anything for granted) and focus on the ingredients of pitching. If you have a poor bullpen, too bad; but you still have to respect the game (remember that getting a hit is difficult) and focus on the ingredients of pitching. Again, **take confidence from your approach;** you know you have the skills to have a good outing regardless of what kind of stuff you have.

> *"The key for me is to forget about results and concentrate on execution."*
> — *Orel Hershiser, Los Angeles Dodgers*

Your body may not have the "feel" you'd like when you come out of the bullpen, but if you lose your head because of it, you're going to have a short outing. By keeping a good mental approach as well as your composure, and trusting what you do have — in other words, playing heads-up — chances are good the "feeling" will come before too long.

So the key to bringing your stuff with you from the bullpen to the game is in your approach to pitching in general. Don't let how you throw in the bullpen determine your confidence. **Confidence is something you carry inside you; it's not in the bullpen.**

One Pitch at a Time: Routines and Releases

In Chapter 4, the **self-control, plan, trust** process was discussed as a way to play the game one pitch at a time. On the mound, this process becomes a routine that you execute before each pitch. When your internal traffic light is green, simply go with your routine. When you hit a yellow or red light, however, you need a way to release whatever happened (such as giving up a two-run double or a fielder booting an easy ground ball). Both routines and releases will be more fully explained in this section.

Prepitch Routines

When you are pitching well you typically have what most pitchers call "rhythm." When you are in your rhythm you are in control of yourself, are totally focused on what you are doing **right now**, and are performing at a comfortable pace. Getting into your rhythm or into "flow" should be one of your primary objectives each time you're on the mound. A prepitch routine can help you do just that. In fact, since your responsibility is to focus on your own performance and play the game one pitch at a time, your routine becomes what you are doing out on the mound.

> *"Don't let luck, chance, and fate become part of your rhythm. Mastering your mental skills gives you the ability to establish rhythm initially, and a way to get it back when you hit a yellow light."*
> — *Steve Rousey, Long Beach State pitching coach*

In its simplest form, **self-control, plan, trust** boils down to breathe, see the ball hit the target, then hit the target. In fact, that could be your routine: "breathe, see it, do it."

Remember, "see it" doesn't necessarily mean you have to actually see the ball going into the target. You might have some "sense" of the ball going there or you might not be into that part of it at all. Somehow get clear about where you want the ball to go.

Here's another example of a straightforward routine:

Self-Control: Step on the rubber when you are ready. Take a slow, steady breath while or before getting your sign from the catcher.

Plan: Visualize the pitch hitting your target.

Trust: Throw the pitch.

You may want to incorporate a cue word or phrase into your routine. For example:

Self-control: Step on the rubber when you are ready.

Plan: Get your sign from the catcher and commit to the pitch.

Trust: Inhale, then say to yourself, "get on top" as you exhale and start your motion.

This phrase can vary with your different pitches. You might say "arm speed" for your change up and "throw through it" on your slider. Also, if you find you are losing concentration in your delivery, you may want to say a word or phrase to yourself such as "free and easy," "nice and fluid," or "finish it" during your motion. Whatever works for you is the right word or phrase to use.

1   2   3   4

Here we see a pitcher working on his routine in the outfield during practice. After getting the ball from the catcher, he adjusts his jersey and "checks in" on his traffic light to make sure he's in **CONTROL** of himself (1). **When he's ready,** he steps onto the rubber (2). Once on the rubber, the pitcher takes a breath as he gets his signal and commits to the **PLAN** for this pitch by visualizing where he wants the ball to go (3). Finally, his "thinking" completed, he **TRUSTS** himself and throws the pitch (4).

Another idea is to think of setting your "plan" as a three-step process which includes **1)** pitch selection, **2)** pitch location and **3)** selecting a specific target that you are throwing to (or through). Your routine (and thought process) then becomes:

Self-control:	Step on the rubber and take a breath.
Plan:	Selection ("change-up") Location ("down and in") Target ("catcher's knee")
Trust:	Throw the pitch.

Many pitchers have found taking two breaths in their routine to be helpful, particularly when they aren't pitching well. We call this the "double breath." The first, taken before stepping onto the rubber, is a self-control breath that helps you let go of the last pitch and any tension or negative thoughts that might have come with it. The second, taken just before beginning your motion, is a "trust" breath that helps you let go of your thinking and frees you to perform. A double breath routine would go something like this:

Self-control: Get the ball back from the catcher and take a good breath either as you walk back to the rubber or while you are standing behind the rubber.

Plan: Step onto the rubber and get your sign.

Trust: Take a breath, then throw the pitch.

Most pitchers find one or two breaths are enough between pitches. You may, of course, end up taking more if you have a yellow or red light and need to release, but more than two during a normal routine is generally a bit much. But remember, whatever works for you is what you should go with.

Don't forget to practice your routine from the stretch position as well as from the wind up. Many pitchers find it comfortable to inhale as they bring their hands up after getting the sign, then exhale as their hands come together and down into the set position. You might then want to visualize your pitch either before checking the runner(s) or the instant before beginning your motion to the plate.

Releases

Your release gets you back to feeling centered and balanced when you have a yellow or red light, or when things might be starting to spiral out of control. (Remember, it really isn't important to distinguish between a yellow and a red light, the main thing to be aware of is that it isn't green!) We listed a number of "Tools For Gaining Control" in Chapter 4. Listed below are some strategies which pitchers have used successfully. You can use one of them or be creative and make up your own.

> *"Some guys will take their glove off, stick it under their arm and rub up the ball. They say to themselves, 'OK, now we'll start all over again'."*
> *— Marcel Lachemann, California Angels manager*

- Brush the dirt off the rubber, "wiping away" whatever negative event just happened.

- Stand behind the rubber and take an extra breath.

- Take your glove off and rub the ball up, "rubbing away" your thoughts of that last pitch.

Mark Langston (above) goes to his focal point to release a negative and regroup before delivering his next pitch so that he isn't throwing more than one pitch at a time (below).

• Pick up the rosin bag, squeeze it a bit to put your emotions into it, then throw it away, throwing your negative emotions away with it.

• Look out to your focal point.

• Take a walk behind the mound to your "toilet" and take some cleansing breaths.

• Take your hat off to "let off some steam" — when you put it back on you are ready to focus on the next pitch.

You may want to have two releases — one for relatively minor adversities such as throwing two straight balls or having a ball slip out of your hand, and one for more significant difficulties such as giving up a home run or watching an infielder botch a simple play that would have ended the inning. For example, you might wipe the dirt off the rubber and take an extra breath after you feel the umpire missed a call, but go back behind the mound and look to your focal point after a two-run double.

Whatever release you use, the key is to have a way to rid yourself of what happened on the last pitch and get totally focused on where the action is — the next pitch.

The Big Game, the Final Inning

What do you do if you are pitching the "big game" or need one more out to clinch a big win? Should you "hump up," "turn it up a notch," or "reach back for something extra?" Of course not! Do what you've practiced from Day One. Do what you did in the bullpen in practice and in the bullpen before you came into the game. You go out and **work the process**: use your routine, take your breaths, use your release just like you have from the first day of practice.

In fact, former Dodger ace Don Sutton said the key to handling World Series pressure is in spring training. He approached each bullpen and each game during the regular season with the respect and focus that he would approach a World Series game. That way he knew exactly what to do when he was playing for the world championship.

Sure, you might be more pumped up than usual in a big game or a big moment, but since you channel that energy into your routine it only helps you play better. **The mental game isn't about getting ready for "The Big One," it's about getting ready for each one.**

Postgame Review

As we mentioned in the last chapter, to learn as much as you can from each outing, take time to evaluate your performance. What did you do well? What did you do poorly? What should you work on between now and your next outing? Getting into the habit of asking yourself questions like these and the ones in Chapter 5 will speed your progress in the game.

The Coach's Box

Coaches, before each game, ask your starting pitcher to show you his routine and his release plan or plans. You then know exactly what to look for during the game. A pitcher's routine and releases become what he is doing on the field, and are important issues to discuss with him between innings and when you take trips to the mound.

7 Hitting: Confidence in the Face of Failure

It's tough enough to hit a baseball traveling between 65 and 100 miles per hour. But when the pitcher changes speeds, makes the ball move in different ways, and does anything else he can to make you miss it or hit it poorly, the challenge grows even larger. It may help to keep in mind that the game's best hitters only succeed about three times in 10. Dealing with a 70 percent failure rate may be baseball's greatest mental challenge. Making one out is bad enough, but the resulting frustration and loss of confidence after making several outs in a row can drive a player crazy. Getting out more often than getting a hit is inevitable, so the important question is, "How can you stay confident in the face of so much failure?" This chapter provides some of the answers.

Hitting Is Difficult

When discussing the mental aspects of hitting, one of the first things to realize is that hitting is difficult. Based on their antics after making an out, many players seem to think hitting is easy and that they should get a base hit each time. We want you to be confident at the plate, but it's also helpful to understand the realities of hitting.

When you understand that hitting is difficult you work harder at it, get more enjoyment from it when you succeed and are less upset when you make outs. Because you are less upset after getting out (we aren't saying you should be happy about it), you are able to objectively look at what happened and learn from what you did. Too often players are overly judgmental and emotional about "failed" at bats, preventing them from learning as much as they can from the opportunity.

When you recognize that hitting is difficult, reduce it to its most basic and simple level. Instead of trying to do too much — such as hitting a home run — your goal should be to put the bat on the ball. Since hitting is already hard, why not try to make it as simple as possible?

The Mission

Another important perspective to keep in mind is the bigger picture your mission (see Chapter 2) helps provide. For example, why do you hit and what do you like about hitting? If you hit because you enjoy it, enjoy it while you are doing it. If you, like many hitters, love the challenge of hitting, keeping that in mind will help you experience less frustration. After all, if it wasn't hard, you wouldn't love it!

> If every time you hit you have the mind-set that you love hitting and you're having fun, the rest of the mental game pretty much takes care of itself. When you are loving it and having fun, you are focused and confident the way you were as a little kid playing whiffle ball in the back yard. When you are filled with those positive emotions there's no room for fears and doubts to get in your way. It can be a tough thing to do, certainly, but the more you are able to keep your love and sense of enjoyment in your head as you hit, the less stress and pressure you are likely to feel while hitting in a game.

Quality At Bats

A major theme of this book is the importance of focusing on things you can control. Focusing on your batting average or other aspects of the game beyond your control wastes mental energy and diminishes your chances of success. As we've stressed all along, you can't control getting a hit. So many important factors — ranging from getting a good pitch to hit to a fielder catching the ball — are outside of your control that it's unrealistic to think you can get a hit any time you want.

This is not to say that hitting is all luck or that you shouldn't be **concerned** with getting hits. Better hitters get more hits and it's important to get hits.

Spend time visualizing yourself getting hits. Instead of focusing on **HOW MANY** hits you get, though, focus on **HOW** to get hits!

> Hitting is a confidence game. Not surprisingly, most players let their confidence be determined by whether or not they are getting hits. The heads-up player, however, bases his confidence on his approach. This idea has been discussed in terms of "working the process." In hitting, working the process translates into "quality at bats." You can't control getting hits, but you can control the quality of your at bats. The more quality at bats you have, the more hits you are likely to get.

Thus, a big part of our answer to our earlier question about remaining confident in the face of so much failure is to focus on what you can control — the process of hitting — rather than the outcome of your at bats. **Evaluate your performances based on the quality of your at bats rather than your outcomes.** Your ability to have quality at bats (something you can control) then becomes the basis for your confidence instead of the number of hits you have (something you can't control).

The rest of this chapter contains ideas you can use and skills you can practice that can enhance the quality of your at bats.

Exercise: **Hitter, Know Yourself**

"Knowing yourself" is one of the keys to having quality at bats. Coaches often tell a player to "stay within yourself." Everyone agrees it's important, but what does it mean? Basically, it means do what you are capable of doing, or don't try to do "too much." The key to staying "within yourself" is knowing what is within your capabilities, what your strengths and weaknesses are, and what type of hitter you are. Only then are you in a position to know if you are within yourself or not.

The first part of staying within yourself involves another common phrase yelled to batters: "get your pitch." Your chances of seeing your pitch are greatly increased if you know what it looks like!

What is "your pitch?" What type of pitch do you like to hit the most? Circle one:

FASTBALL	**CURVEBALL**
SLIDER	**CHANGE-UP**
SPLIT-FINGER	**OTHER (explain)**

Next, where in the strike zone do you hit the ball best? In the strike zone below, shade the area in which you are most likely to hit the ball well.

How would you describe yourself as a hitter? or What type of a hitter are you?

When you are hitting well, what are you trying to do with the ball?

When you are hitting well, where does the ball go? Using the diagram on the right, shade in the area on the field where most of your well-hit balls go.

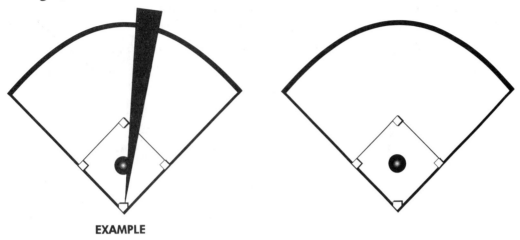

EXAMPLE

Hitting One Pitch at a Time

Another important aspect of having a quality at bat is playing the game one pitch at a time. In the next three sections we'll talk about how the self-control, plan, trust model applies to hitting.

Be in Control

In many ways, the basic challenge of hitting is to be in control of yourself enough so that you remain relaxed and focused despite the potential pressures and fears of going one-on-one with the pitcher while everyone in the ballpark watches.

From a mechanical standpoint, it's apparent whether or not a batter is in control of himself by observing his ability to take his stride but keep his weight and hands back until he starts his swing. Also, the hitter who is in control of himself only swings at good pitches. When a coach tells you to have "discipline" at the plate, he's really saying you need to be in control of yourself enough to see the ball and make a sound decision on whether or not you should swing.

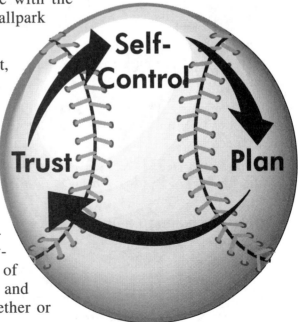

Frank Thomas, widely recognized as the best all-around hitter in the game today, is an excellent example of a player in control of himself at the plate. His high average and frequent walks are a testament to his ability to clear his mind and relax when he's hitting. In fact, he works at staying so relaxed in his stance that someone could easily slide the bat right out of his hands.

Many ideas for improving your self-control were presented in Chapter 3. Keeping your mission in mind, having fun, taking quality breaths, using a routine, having a focal point and developing a way to "release" negative thoughts and events can be used before or during an at bat for this purpose. How these methods of self-control can be worked into your hitting will be discussed throughout this chapter.

Have A Plan

To play the game one pitch at a time, it's important to have a plan on each pitch. If you know what you are up there to do, the chances of "giving away" the at bat decrease and the chances of having a quality at bat increase.

Your answers to the questions we asked earlier in this chapter provide critical information about what your plan should be. Generally speaking, **do the things you do when you are hitting well.** If, for example, you are a right-handed hitter and hit the ball to center and right-center when you are hitting well, your plan should be to hit the ball to center and right-center most of the time.

When determining your plan for an at bat, always remember that **HITTING IS DIFFICULT.** As we discussed earlier, if you realize that something is difficult you try to simplify it. In hitting, that means the primary focus of your plan is to hit the ball. Listen to these great hitters talk about what they were trying to do at the plate:

- **Pete Rose (4,256 hits)** — "See the ball, hit the ball. That's it. If you get more complicated than that you're making it more difficult than it needs to be."

- **Stan Musial (.331 over 22 seasons)** — "My idea of hitting was get the fat part of the bat on the ball and hitting the ball where it was pitched."

- **Billy Williams (Hall of Famer)** — "I just watched it come in, took a good swing at it, and tried to hit it with the fat of the bat. Where it went from there I didn't give a damn."

THE TASK OF HITTING
IS TO PUT THE FAT PART OF THE BAT ON THE BALL

It was smart of these hitters to simplify hitting, but it was brilliant of them to keep it simple for as long as they did. Get into the habit of asking yourself before each at bat: what am I going to do at the plate? Your plan may simply be to "hit the ball," "see the ball," or "stay back." It may also include some direction you are trying to hit it such as up the middle, to the opposite field or to your pull side.

Many hitters think "up the middle" if they are going to try to hit the ball in a particular direction. The hole up the middle is the biggest in the infield and thinking "right back at the pitcher" provides the best opportunity to hit a fair ball. This orientation also helps keep sound mechanics in order. In fact, many hitters try to drive the ball into the opposite field gap because this thought keeps their heads down and shoulders in. Of course, what you are trying to do at the plate varies with your strengths as a hitter and the game situation.

Two additional questions you might want to ask yourself as you figure out your plan are:

1) What pitch am I looking for?
2) Where am I looking for the pitch to be?

It often works out that the more clear you are on what "your pitch" is, the more often you see it.

Although you likely will have one basic plan most of the time, your plan varies depending on how good you feel at the plate, the count, how well you are seeing the ball, the game situation, the score, the weather, any injuries you might have, how hard the pitcher is throwing, and the style and strengths of the pitcher.

> *"It was a constant battle of adjustments. Every at bat, every time in the batter's box there was a game plan."*
> *— former Boston Red Sox all-star Carl Yastrzemski*

For example, what will you be looking for when you are ahead in the count 2-and-0 or 3-and-1? What is your plan when you have two strikes or there's a man on second with nobody out? Thinking these questions through in advance and practicing them in batting practice improves your chances of succeeding in a game.

In summary, your plan is determined by your answers to one or more of the following questions:

1) What am I trying to do?
2) Where am I trying to hit the ball?
3) What pitch am I looking for?
4) Where in the strike zone am I looking for the ball?

A few examples of plans at the plate might include:

- "see it and hit it"
- "hit it hard up the middle"
- "put the fat part of the bat on the ball"
- "hit a hard ground ball"
- "fastball out over the plate, hit it right back at him"
- "breaking ball, middle of the plate on out, drive it the other way"
- "look for a pitch up in the strike zone"

> Whatever your plan, the main point is to know what you are trying to do at the plate and **COMMIT** to that plan. Hitters often go to the plate not knowing what they are trying to do, or trying to do something they aren't really capable of doing (such as pulling the ball out of the park). In other words, they either have no idea or a bad idea.

It's a Matter of Trust

Another key to a quality at bat is trust. A hitter only has one-half second — about as long as it normally takes you to say the word "fastball" out loud — to see the ball, make a decision on whether or not to swing, and, if he decides to swing, get the bat to where the ball is. Contrary to what you might think, though, the biggest problem for hitters is not being late with their decisions and their swings.

Most mistakes in hitting result from deciding on a pitch too soon. The source of this problem? Lack of trust. If you don't trust yourself, your stride is big and "loud," your weight lunges toward the pitcher, your front shoulder flies open, and you start your swing before you've really had a chance to see the ball. When you see hitters swing at bad balls it's a pretty good indication that they aren't trusting themselves and they're out of control.

As a hitter, trust that your hands will come through, trust that you can get around on a guy, and trust that you will have enough power in your swing without "muscling up."

A hitter who trusts himself automatically does a number of things vital to good hitting. First, he's not in a rush to start his swing, so he has a chance to **see the baseball.** Hitting is first and foremost a visual skill, so this benefit of trust is critical. Hitters who are hitting well talk about how big the ball is and how well they see it. Struggling hitters report cases of "small ball" and that the pitcher appears to be throwing peas. Although some pitchers hide the ball better than others, the size of the ball never changes so we can safely say that **the difference between the ball looking big or small is a result of what is going on behind the hitter's eyes rather than in front of them!**

Trust also eliminates obstacles to clear thinking. As discussed previously, doubt, anxiety and tension cloud your mind and keep you from making good decisions both before and during the pitch. We feel it's best to refer to what happens during the time the ball is on its way to the plate as "reacting" rather than "thinking," but there's no doubt that a quick, clear decision about whether to take a hack or not must be made at some point. A trusting mind-set clears the way for this to happen. You don't have much time, but trust yourself, you've got more time than you think.

Finally, trust keeps your swing fluid. Tension, brought on by fear and doubt, is one of a hitter's biggest enemies. Muscles move most efficiently when re-relaxed; a tense muscle is a slow muscle. Actually, when we get "tense" it means we are tightening muscles that don't need to be tightened. For example, if your biceps are tightened as you swing, they work against you. Your triceps must then overcome not only the weight of the bat, but also the re-

> "I wait and wait and let the ball get right on top of me and just swing with a loose grip."
> — *Tony Gwynn,*
> **National League batting champ**

sistance created by your biceps as you swing. Thus, your motion is slower and less fluid than if your biceps were relaxed.

Most hitters talk about the need to feel relaxed at the plate. Relax and trust your body — it knows what muscles are needed to execute a good swing.

The Eyes Have It

As noted earlier, hitting is first and foremost a visual skill. Regardless of what you do mechanically, if you don't see the ball you aren't going to hit it. Once again, preparation is a key element in your success. What you do with your eyes before the ball is thrown has a great deal to do with how well you see the ball when it is thrown.

What do you look at when you are in the batter's box waiting for the pitcher to throw the ball? Most hitters understand the mechanics of their swing pretty well, but few have any idea what their eyes do when they are hitting. Since vision is the most important aspect of hitting, this isn't a good idea.

Most of the best hitters say that they pick out a spot on the pitcher, such as the emblem on his cap or somewhere on his chest, and use a "soft" focus on it while the pitcher is getting the signs and starting his windup. Just before the pitcher's hand reaches his release point, they shift to a "hard" focus on the pitcher's release point. Hitters refer to the spot from which the ball comes as the "box" or the "window." Then they track the ball as best they can as it comes toward the plate.

With this in mind, it's critical to know where a pitcher's release point is. To do this, study the pitcher as he warms up and also as he throws to other hitters. Intently watching a pitcher and visualizing yourself facing him can improve your efficiency in your shift from him to his release point. This is a big part of doing your "homework."

The reason you focus on a spot on the pitcher is to set your eyes at the distance the ball will be from you when it comes into view. If you shift to the release point too soon, your eyes focus on a point past the pitcher (your eyes can't focus on something that isn't there, so they focus on a distant object). When the ball does appear, your eyes must readjust to the nearer distance, taking time that you don't have.

This eye pattern is sensible and helps many hitters, but you need to find out what works best for you. You may find that thinking about what your eyes are doing clutters your mind and makes it hard to hit at first, but as you settle in to a pattern that works for you, your performance will improve.

What causes the ball to look smaller when you aren't hitting well? "Small ball" happens for many reasons, and most likely results from several factors. Try this one: put the book down and pretend that you are really nervous or scared. What did you do with your eyes? When we are nervous or scared, our eyes tend to shift rapidly from one spot to another, not really focusing on anything for very long. If your eyes are jumping around while you're in the batter's box you aren't going to see the ball very well.

Further, if your eyes reach the release point late, the ball has already traveled several feet before you get any kind of look at it. The shorter time to look at the pitch makes it seem much faster than it actually is, making the ball appear much smaller.

Finally, your eye movements are controlled by muscles. Thus, if you have any excess tension in your face, the efficiency of your eye movement is hindered. In other words, your eyes don't work as well when you are nervous or tight.

The cure for small ball boils down to trust. The calmness that results from trust can steady your focus and relax your eye muscles. Add a sound eye pattern of shifting from a spot on the pitcher to the release point and you'll be giving yourself your best chance for success.

Pregame Batting Practice

Batting practice is important. It serves as a short practice session prior to a game and provides an opportunity to tune up and tune in. It's a chance to get comfortable with the field, feel the ball come off the bat and reinforce your mechanics. Contrary to the trap many players fall into, however, hitting every ball on the nose and ripping it all over the park isn't the most important thing in batting practice. What is important is the approach you take to batting practice.

Batting practice is the time to practice doing what you are going to do in the game and focus on the ingredients of hitting: get prepared to hit, have a plan or a mission in mind when you step in, execute that plan. Your mission may be to hit the ball the other way, keep your head down on the ball, or simply to see the ball and hit it. The key is to have something specific in mind when you step in, some clear purpose for going to the plate.

What you don't want to do is hop in and go through the motions, or just "see what happens." That doesn't help you and it may hurt you.

Have a mission in mind before you step into the cage for batting practice. Be prepared to hit; don't hit to prepare.

You often see a guy run in to the cage to take his hacks without being ready mentally or physically. Because he isn't ready, he has a bad round and gets increasingly upset with each pitch he fouls off or hits on the handle of the bat. As he stomps off, he's thinking it's not going to be his day!

If he had prepared himself better, he might have had a better attitude after leaving the cage. Don't let your performance in batting practice determine how your day at the plate is going to go — unless, of course, you had a great batting practice!

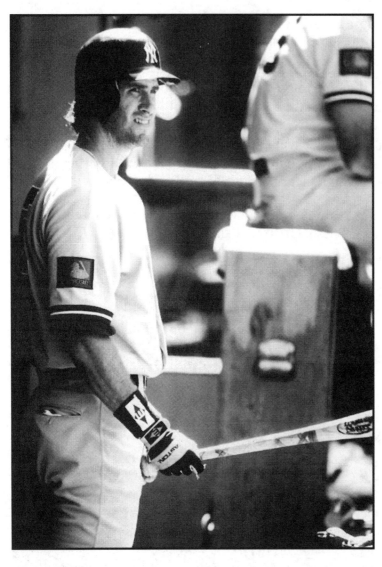

Paul O'Neill is pre-pared to hit long be-fore he reaches the plate. Quality prepara-tion can reduce the number of at bats you "throw away" each season.

Batting practice is simply part of the preparation process. If you hit well, great; but if it doesn't go well, use your mental skills to evaluate what happened and get yourself focused on what you need to do during the game. It's nice to walk out of the cage with that little buzz that comes from stinging line drives all over the yard. In the real world, however, that doesn't happen every day. For one thing, much of how well you hit in batting practice depends on the quality of the pitches you get. As usual, a lot of it is beyond your control! Besides, the floaters you get in batting practice are very different from what you'll see during the game.

So, just like your at bats in a ball game, it's critical to prepare yourself for your time in the cage so that you'll have a quality batting practice session.

Prepare yourself physically by warming up well before you step into the cage: don't hit to get loose, get loose to hit. Just as important, prepare mentally by having a plan or a mission for each round or pitch. While waiting for your turn in the cage, visualize what you want to do when you get in there. Quality preparation builds confidence. We will talk more about the mental game of batting practice in Chapter 9.

During the Game

One of the most important things to do before and during the game is study the opposing pitcher. Good hitters are gluttons for information: they always look for clues to help them solve the puzzle each pitcher represents. Ty Cobb, a lifetime .366 hitter, said that "batting is like the study of a crime, observing little details that are of immense importance."

The important information to pick up includes what pitches he throws, where his release point is, how his ball moves, what he throws in different counts and his strategy against hitters that are similar to you. Use this information as you determine your plan at the plate.

The Pre-At Bat Routine

One of the best ways to enhance the consistency and quality of your at bats is to have a pre-at bat routine. Think of a pre-at bat routine like a funnel, channeling your thoughts down to where they need to be to give you your best chance of being successful. In this section, we'll give you some ideas about what might go into a pre-at bat routine and an opportunity to develop one of your own.

Getting Started

When does an at bat begin? One idea we stressed in the chapter on mental preparation was to set a definite point before a game where you became a ballplayer. The same idea holds true for an at bat: pick a set time before an at bat that you become a hitter.

You can choose anything to signify the start of an at bat. One of the most popular and effective is when you pick up your batting helmet. Instead of mindlessly putting on your helmet while you're talking to the batboy or a teammate, make the act of putting on your helmet the start of your at bat — you're putting on your hitting head. From

> "I can't control the pitcher, the ball, the fielders or the crowd, so I must be in control of myself. My routine not only prepares me physically, but mentally creates the same frame of mind every time."
> — *Tim Salmon, California Angels, 1993 AL Rookie of the Year*

that point on your thoughts are centered on this next at bat, and they are all positive (i.e., "I'm going to smoke it this time"). Deciding that your turn at the plate begins when you put on your helmet can enhance the quality of your batting practice and reduce the number of at bats you "throw away" each season. Similarly, a lot of hitters make putting on their batting gloves a big deal. As you put them on, tell yourself you are putting on the ultimate hitter and that you will "trust your hands."

Other ideas include when you pick up your bat or step out of the dugout. The main point is to designate the time well before you step into the batter's box when the at bat begins for you.

In the Hole and on Deck

The time when you are third up or next up is also important. Again, the idea is to have some things you do that help funnel you in and keep you from going to the plate unprepared. Some suggestions for what to do when you are in the hole and on deck are listed below. (Remember, we're not saying you have to do all of these, we're giving you some ideas.)

- Get your body ready. The first thing you need to do as your turn at the plate approaches is get your body ready to do battle. This usually entails some stretching and swinging of a bat. Don't cut corners on this one: if you neglect your body in the on-deck area, it is likely to neglect you at the plate.

- Study the pitcher. You can get some good views of him when you are out of the dugout. See every pitch he throws.

- Get clear on your plan. Remind yourself of what you are going to try to do and what you are going to look for.

- Pretend that you are at bat. Imagine you are at the plate while a teammate is hitting to help time the pitcher's delivery and focus on his release point.

- Remind yourself of any mechanical pointers that are helpful to you. You don't want to be thinking mechanics in the batter's box, so give your body some final instructions before you go up there.

- Visualize pitches coming in from the pitcher and taking swings at pitches in different parts of the strike zone. Regardless of how clear the images are, attempting to see the pitcher's release point and the movement on his ball sharpen your concentration and help prepare you for what you will see at the plate.

- Take a deep breath or two and check your body for tension. This is always a good idea.

- Doing a particular stretch, take a deep breath and focus on the air as it comes in and out.

- Take a breath and raise your posture to that of a totally confident hitter.

- While walking to the plate, tell yourself that with each step your concentration on the baseball clicks in deeper.

At the Plate: Hitting One Pitch at a Time

Your preparation is wasted if your focus and trust are lost when you are at the plate. Here are some ideas of things you can do just outside the box or as you step in to get yourself where you want to be — confident and focused on the baseball.

- Take a breath.

- Remind yourself of your plan. "Hit it hard up the middle."

- Combine a deep breath with a cue word or phrase. For example, take a deep breath and think "stay back and see the ball" as you exhale.

- Smooth the dirt in the batter's box with your foot before you step in, wiping away all negative thoughts, any previous bad at bats, and all other players who have stood there during the game.

- Step into the box the same way each time. For example, plant your back foot, then your front foot, then tap the plate. Finally, direct your focus to the pitcher and the baseball.

- Look at your focal point.

- Focus on the label of your bat. Let that action clear your mind.

When you hit well you are not really thinking about anything in the batter's box. Other times, however, you are up there thinking about everything. As we mentioned in the Chapter 4, it can be very helpful to have one word or phrase that you will **CHOOSE** to think instead of leaving those all-important final thoughts to **CHANCE.** This thought should capture what you are trying to do at the plate and will keep you from thinking anything that isn't helpful. Examples include, "see the ball, hit the ball," "right back at him," and "relax and trust it."

Play with these ideas in practice to determine what works best for you and whether you need to do something between each pitch, when you step in the box for the first time, or whenever you feel you need some help.

1

2

3

These three photos illustrate a batter using his routine as he steps into the batter's box. First he wipes the box clean to clear any negative thoughts he might have from his last at bat and to give himself a chance to feel that he's in **CONTROL (1).** He takes a deep breath, focuses his attention on the fat part of the bat and reminds himself of his **PLAN:** "Drive the ball up the middle" **(2).** When he plants his left foot, it's time to **TRUST (3).** If you have access to a copy of Ken Burns' PBS documentary *Baseball,* check out Inning 9 of the series and watch Carlton Fisk execute a nearly identical routine just before hitting his game-winning home run in Game 6 of the 1975 World Series.

Building Your Routine

Now that we've given you some ideas, use the funnel on the following page to write down one or two things you'll do at each point that will help funnel you to where you want to be at the plate — focused on the baseball. Again, the goal is to help you feel and think the way that will help you the most.

As you work through the exercise, think about what has worked for you in the past. Keep in mind that some players use a very structured pre-at bat routine with a lot of things to do at particular times, while others are better off with only one or two things to do sometime before each at bat.

Example

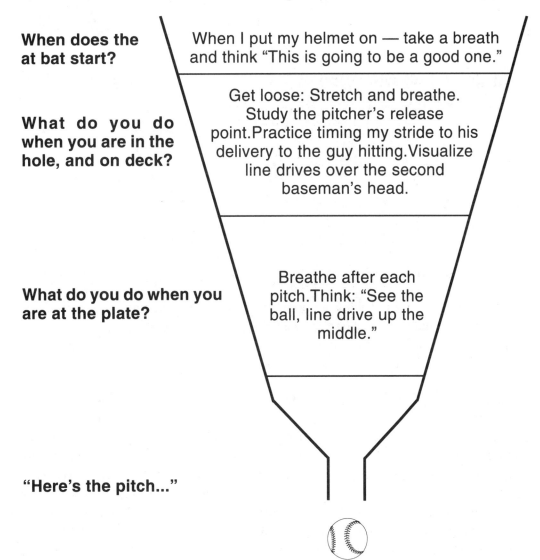

When does the at bat start?

When I put my helmet on — take a breath and think "This is going to be a good one."

What do you do when you are in the hole, and on deck?

Get loose: Stretch and breathe. Study the pitcher's release point.Practice timing my stride to his delivery to the guy hitting.Visualize line drives over the second baseman's head.

What do you do when you are at the plate?

Breathe after each pitch.Think: "See the ball, line drive up the middle."

"Here's the pitch..."

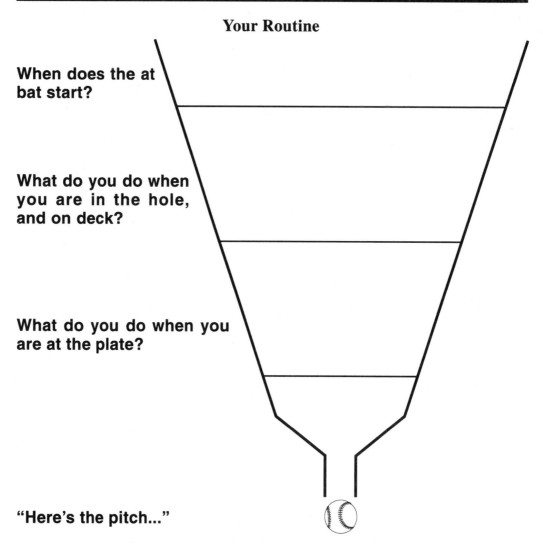

Your Routine

When does the at bat start?

What do you do when you are in the hole, and on deck?

What do you do when you are at the plate?

"Here's the pitch..."

It's likely that you'll want to change or adjust your routine over time as you discover what seems to be the most helpful to you. Don't forget, if you are leading off an inning you'll need to be comfortable working through your routine rapidly.

Releases: Getting It Back Together at the Plate

Despite your focus and preparation, a reality of hitting is that something can happen up there that will throw you off and start you spiraling out of control. Some of these "yellow lights" include swinging and missing at a bad pitch, fouling off a great pitch to hit, a bad call by the umpire, being "frozen" by a particularly nasty pitch, failing to execute a bunt, having a pitch just miss your head, being overpowered by a fastball, hearing a stupid comment from the opposing dugout and having a teammate picked off base. You might even recognize that you weren't really prepared to be up there in the first place!

What are your yellow lights at the plate? What can throw you off into a spiral?

> It's imperative for you to learn to let go of anything negative that happened and refocus on the next pitch when you recognize you have lost control. Countless at bats are wasted each season because hitters allow something that happened on a previous pitch to carry over into the rest of the at bat. A heads-up player doesn't throw away at bats like that.

Here are some ideas for how to release your tension and distractions and get yourself refocused on the next pitch:

- Take an extra breath.

- Look out at your focal point.

- Talk yourself through it. "I'm OK. I can't do anything about that now. Let it go, relax, and focus in on the next pitch."

- Turn away from the plate for a moment.

- Redo your batting gloves. As you lift the Velcro strap you are taking off what happened on the last pitch, and as you refasten it you are tightening down your focus on the next pitch.

- Pick up some dirt, squeeze it to put your frustration into it, then toss the dirt and your frustration behind you.

- Put your hand on your head and adjust your helmet. Think of screwing your head back down.

> *"An at bat is a terrible thing to waste."*
> *— Joe Maddon, California Angels coach*

Many leagues have a speed up rule that doesn't allow you to step out of the batter's box between pitches. That makes it even more important to have a release plan to go to because you don't have much time to turn it around. Most of the above ideas can be done easily without stepping out of the box. When you get a yellow light, take some time, take a breath and stay in control.

Slumps

You might expect a section on slumps to be lengthy in a book on the mental aspects of baseball. Slumps, or at least "dry spells," happen to everyone eventually and are among the toughest challenges you will face in the game. Actually, though, this book is about how to develop the mental skills needed to play your best baseball, not about how to avoid playing badly.

If you start working on this material over the winter, practice it during regular and preseason workouts, and use it in all of your games, you'll not only have fewer slumps, but you'll also have plenty of ideas to go to whenever you are struggling. Our advice on slumps is: **DON'T WAIT FOR A SLUMP TO HAPPEN BEFORE YOU START WORKING ON YOUR MENTAL GAME!**

Also, don't go immediately to your mechanics when you're struggling. Focus instead on the quality of your at bats from a mental standpoint. Mechanical problems such as lunging and pulling off the ball are usually caused by ineffective thinking. Go right to the source of the problem; don't just tinker with the symptom.

Additional thoughts to consider when you feel like you are in a slump:

- Do or redo the exercises in this and all previous chapters (especially at the end of Chapter 1 and in this chapter). They will help you get back to thinking productive and positive thoughts. There's a good chance you are struggling because you've gotten away from doing the things that usually lead to your best at bats.

- Keep it simple. Have a basic plan and stick with it.

- Focus on the quality of your at bats. Again, you can't control getting hits but you can control the quality of your at bats. You might go 0-for-4 in a game but go 3-for-4 with quality at bats. Keep track of your quality at bats average instead of your batting average.

- Keep it one at bat at a time. Don't think about how you are 0-for-13 or 2-for-20. That just results in your trying to get four hits in one turn at the plate. You are now 0-for-0. You have no control over the past or the future so get your head in the present. Use your routine and work the process.

- Choose your words carefully. Don't admit to being in a slump. Focus instead on how you are "due" to get a base hit. If you let yourself buy into the "I can't hit" or "I stink" mentality you're digging yourself a deeper hole. Talk to yourself the way you'd talk to your best friend who isn't hitting well. Remember, if you spend your time thinking about hitting poorly, you're going to hit poorly.

- Go back to what was working for you earlier. From both a mental and mechanical standpoint, getting out of a slump is usually more a matter of going to what has worked well for you in the past than it is going to something new. When you're struggling, everyone in the ballpark gives you tips on what to do. Although your friend's dad might be right that a new position for your hands might help you break out, the most likely place to find help is in your own past.

- Read the journal you've been keeping all along. "Oops! You know, I've been meaning to write some of these things down..." Wouldn't it be nice to have a journal you could read now that would tell you what you were doing when you were playing well? You'd be surprised how much good information you forget and how helpful it can be when you hit a skid.

- Give your teammates some positive energy and support. Making an extra effort to be supportive of your teammates not only helps them, but you'll get back what you give out. Instead of wallowing in self-pity, beating yourself up and overanalyzing your mechanics, channel your energy in a genuine, positive way. Before long, good things will start happening to you.

- Try less. A common reaction to a slump is for a hitter to try harder. After all, that's the American way: if you fail, try harder. The result is a lot of extra batting practice and a lot of tension at the plate as you really "bear down." Extra batting practice and work on your swing can help a great deal and often help batters get back on track. If you've tried working harder and haven't had success, however, try working less. Skip batting practice, goof around a little and see how relaxed you can get at the plate.

Evaluating the Quality of Your At Bats

The focus of this chapter has been on helping you deal with the "failure" you experience as a hitter by encouraging you to focus more on the process of hitting rather than the outcomes of your at bats.

Since the mental aspects of hitting revolve around the idea of having quality at bats, it's important to get into the habit of assessing the quality of your at bats. This habit will help you in the difficult switch from basing your confidence the number of hits you have to how well you "worked the process."

> **Here's an example of how a batter focusing on having quality at bats might assess his day at the plate:**
> - Name — Steve Bruno
> - Plate appearances during the game — 5
> - In control of myself — 4-for-5
> - Had a clear plan and stuck to it — 4-for-5
> - Saw the ball well— 3-for-5
> - Made solid contact — 2-for-5
> - Overall quality at bats — 3-for-5
> - Base hits — 0-for-5
>
> **Did Steve have a successful day?**

Listed on the following page are some questions you can ask yourself after each at bat and/or each game. Record your answers in a journal as often as possible.

- Did you study the pitcher from the dugout?

- Did you use your routine?

- Were you in control of yourself before each pitch?

- What were your yellow lights?

- What did you do to get yourself back under control when you had a yellow or red light?

- Did you have a clear and simple plan on each pitch? What plan or plans did you use?

- Were you committed to your plan or did you just pay it "lip service?"

- Did you trust yourself or were you anxious and jump out at the ball?

- What was your "quality at bat average" for the game? (You may, have been 0-for-4 in hits, for example, but 2-for-4 in quality at bats.)

The Coach's Box

You determine much of the success a player has in focusing on the quality of his at bats instead of the number of hits he gets. The actions you praise and the questions you ask tell your players what you think is important. Be relentless in complimenting hitters when they have quality at bats, especially when they **don't** result in base hits. When you speak with the team between innings or at the end of the game, talk through one or two at bats where you felt a player kept himself under control and "worked the process" well. In particular, look for times when a hitter had to deal with adversity such as a bad call by the umpire or swinging at a bad pitch. You can't expect your players to think process if you talk outcome.

Fielding and Baserunning

Although most of the game revolves around the duel between the pitcher and hitter, defense and baserunning also play a vital role in determining every game's outcome. Defensively, you aren't helping your team if you give the other team a run with your glove for every run you drive in with your bat.

Offensively, putting pressure on the opposition and taking an extra base when it's there — which is as much a matter of alertness and anticipation as it is speed — will make you a major asset to any ballclub. In this chapter, the ideas presented throughout the book are applied to fielding and baserunning to help improve your skills in both areas.

Fielding: "Hit it to me"

The challenge of fielding is to be focused and confident on each pitch. In other words, play the game one pitch at a time just as you would if you were pitching or hitting. There will be times when this comes easily for you, but there also will be plenty of times when you aren't totally focused on playing defense.

You might be in position physically, but your head is on your last at bat, your next at bat, an error you just made, the great play you just made, your social calendar, how your favorite NFL team will do this year or some other mental tangent that takes your mind everywhere but where it needs to be in order for you to play your best defense. **When you are playing defense, you want to be in a peak performance zone, not the Twilight Zone.**

When you are focused and in control of yourself before a pitch you not only get the best jump you can on the ball, but keeping your composure while making the play is less difficult. The game seems to move along at a comfortable pace. When you are in control of yourself before the play, your chances of staying in control during the play are greatly enhanced.

If you haven't focused or are spiraling out of control before a pitch, not only do you fail to get a good jump on a ball hit your way, but you also are more likely to panic while the ball is on its way to you. If you feel surprised when the ball is hit to you or everything seems to be in fast forward you probably are not playing one pitch at a time.

San Francisco Giants third baseman Matt Williams prepares to make a play. The challenge of fielding is to be focused and confident on each pitch.

It's so easy for your mind to wander that your real opponent isn't always the other team — **the real enemy is boredom!** You must have total focus on each pitch even though the kids chasing foul balls are getting more action than you are. When your team is up to bat but you're not likely to hit until the next inning, you can kick back a little, but in the field, the slightest lapse may result in anything from a slow reaction at best to, at worst, an error that costs your team the game. It's funny how the ball seems to find the player who isn't focused or doesn't want the ball hit to him.

In short, fielding requires a mind-set that says "hit it to me." When you want the ball you anticipate what you will do when the ball is hit to you; you are confident, focused, in control and move to the ball in an aggressive but relaxed way. Our discussion of fielding therefore, centers on helping you consistently want the ball to be hit to you.

The Mission

The place to start a discussion on fielding is with your mission. What do you want your reputation as a fielder to be, for example, and what must you do to earn that reputation?

Great performers in any field love what they do, at least in some way. If you are passionate about something, you not only do it often, but with full focus and intensity. In short, you do it with purpose.

Review your mission: why do you play and what do you want to accomplish in baseball? What do you love about fielding? Where does pride show up in your fielding?

Passion, joy and fun are instrumental in the way future Hall of Famer Ozzie Smith plays defense. "The whole thing in jazz is being free to create, to know something so well that you can improvise. I think of playing shortstop that way."

Exercise: **Fielder, Know Yourself**

The next step in enhancing your performance as a fielder is gaining an understanding of what kind of a fielder you are now. An analysis of your strengths and weaknesses will identify sources of confidence and provide direction to your efforts in practice.

What are your strengths and weaknesses as a fielder? Consider the following elements of defensive play: backhand plays, forehand plays, coming in on balls, going back on balls, fly balls, reading the ball off the bat, taking the proper angle to the ball, first-step quickness, tension in hands, short hops, double-play balls, blocking balls, throwing accuracy, throwing strength, defensive strategy, throwing to correct base, trusting yourself, and ability to stay focused and play one pitch at a time.

Strengths	**Weaknesses**

When you are fielding your best, what is your attitude or mind-set?

When you are fielding your best, what thoughts go through your mind before each pitch? (If your answer is "nothing," put down what you would be saying to yourself if you were saying something.)

When you are struggling in the field, what thoughts go through your mind before each pitch?

The main purpose of these questions is to help you be aware of the importance of your thoughts. Choose to think good thoughts regardless of what you are feeling. It doesn't guarantee great play, but it gives you your best chance of playing well.

Playing Defense One Pitch at a Time

In Chapter 4 we introduced the self-control, plan, trust model and provided some examples of how to apply it to fielding. In this section, the three steps are discussed and applied to fielding in detail.

Get Control

The foundation for good defense is being in control of yourself or having a green light. You can't think clearly (plan) or trust yourself if you have a "monkey on your back" chirping in your ear about how badly you played that last ball. If you don't get rid of him, that monkey can cause you to get a slow jump or misplay the next ball; then you've got a gorilla to deal with!

"Don't hit it to me!"

If you make a mistake in the field, use your mental skills to get the "monkey off your back" before he turns into a gorilla.

Part of being in control is being relaxed. You want to be aggressive and intense, but you can't afford excess tension in your body. Many players have balls pop out of their gloves because their hands are too tight. Good fielders have "soft hands" that are loose and relaxed.

Use the time between pitches to get yourself relaxed and under control; that's where much of the action is on defense. If you don't get your self under control **between** pitches it's unlikely you'll be in control **during** them. We'll talk later about using your breath, a prepitch routine and some type of "release" to help you stay in control.

Have a Plan

> Success in fielding boils down to anticipation. Good defensive players always know the situation and know what they are going to do with the ball if it is hit to them. There are many things to consider when deciding what to do with a batted ball, including knowing the speed of the runners, the score, the batter's position in the lineup, the number of outs, the type of pitcher you have on the mound, and your strengths and weaknesses as a fielder.

Anticipation is the key to getting a "good jump" on the ball. Your first step often determines whether or not you make the play. Top defensive players are taking that first step just as, or even slightly before, the ball is hit. They use the time between pitches to consider the variables that could come together on this pitch. As the pitch is made, they tune in to the cues — the type of pitch thrown, its location, the way the batter is swinging at the ball — that tip-off where the ball will be hit. The result is a good jump on the ball. Without this anticipation, he is likely to freeze or even move the wrong way when "all of the sudden" a ball is hit toward him.

Solidify your plan and sharpen your sense of anticipation by visualizing balls being hit to you between pitches. The best fielders do this naturally. A game-saving catch by former Red Sox outfielder Dwight Evans in the sixth game of the 1975 World Series shows what can happen with visualization. *"Just before the pitch I was going over in my mind what I would do if the ball went into the stands. I saw the ball going in and myself diving after it — and then it really happened."*

If you can, between pitches see balls hit to your right, left and over your head. See if you can "feel" yourself making the play. Just trying to do it will increase your level of concentration.

Communication among teammates is another important element in fielding. Talking and signaling your plans for how to play a particular hitter, what bunt coverage is on, who has the base on a steal, how many outs there are, and if a pick-off play is on, prepares your mind and enables you to react instead of thinking during the play.

Planning and communicating are especially important when you are in a bit of a fielding slump or recognize that you aren't focused on each pitch. Talking about where the batter hit the ball last time, for example, gets your focus away from yourself and occupies your mind with important information. When you anticipate and visualize the next play you're less likely to "space out" or think negatively, and more likely to develop an overwhelming desire to have the ball hit to you.

Trust It

The mind-set that says "Hit it to me" is a trusting mind-set. A trusting mind-set opens the door to playing good defense.

> When you are trusting yourself you see the ball better and you're better able to wait and react to the baseball. Not that we're saying you should wait on balls hit to you — defensive players generally need to be aggressive — but when you trust yourself you can "aggressively wait" for the ball. Although you may be charging in on a ground or fly ball, the play seems to be happening slowly and you can choose the hop you get on a ground ball or the way you catch a ball in the air.

Trust allows you to stay soft as the ball reaches you. Sudden tensing of the hands just before the ball reaches the glove results in many errors. Tension is caused by a lack of trust. Your hands must be soft — void of tension — to give yourself your best chance of catching the baseball.

Once you have the ball in your hands, trust allows you to make a throw that is confident and free. When you trust yourself you focus clearly on your target and let the ball go with a full, fluid action. You don't try to "aim" the ball, and you aren't "careful," you **let it go.**

When you have trouble throwing, it's likely that you aren't picking out a specific target and throwing **through** that target. Instead, you probably have a scattered, erratic focus on a general target area that you hope to throw **to.**

Getting to Trust: The Circle of Focus

Your goal on defense is to overcome all the possible distractions and play one pitch at a time by having yourself under control, anticipating what might happen on the next pitch and trusting yourself. After each pitch, though, it's important to step back a bit and relax. Keeping a full focus through an entire game or even an inning can burn you out and leave you unable to fully focus late in the game. After this brief relaxation period, the whole process begins again for the next pitch.

> An idea that helps players with the process of focusing on the pitch and letting it go afterwards is the "circle of focus." While waiting for a pitch to be thrown, imagine a small circle in front of you. When you step into that circle, focus intently. After the pitch, step back to free your mind and let it wander a bit. Thus, as the pitcher begins or is about to begin his motion, step into the circle. When the pitch is over, step back out.

Experiment with the timing of when you should step into your circle. As the Angels' Damion Easley points out, "If you get into the circle too soon, your mind can start to wander."

When you step into your **circle of focus** you connect with the pitch. Between pitches, step back and allow your concentration to relax for a moment.

Exactly where you focus during the pitch depends on your personal preference and the position you are playing. Outfielders, for example, may follow the flight of the pitch all the way, while infielders are more likely to focus on the plate and follow the pitch with their peripheral vision. Catchers, like hitters, need to shift their focus to the pitcher's release point.

What is your focus when you are playing at your best? It's a good idea to know the answer to that question so you can use your best focus during times you are distracted or aren't confident in the field.

Prepitch Routines

Stepping in and out of your circle of focus serves as your prepitch routine. Throughout the book, a routine has been described as a mental funnel, channeling your thoughts and focus from wherever they are to where you want them to be on each pitch.

When you are pumped up to play defense and are focused on each pitch, you may not need a routine. When you aren't at the top of your game because of a bad at bat, a fielding slump, or the game is on the line, you'll want something to go to that will help you get rid of those yellow lights.

Here are a few things you could work into a prepitch routine:

- **Take a breath.** The breath helps you get control and keep your focus on the present moment.

- **Say a short word or phrase to yourself.** "Hit it to me" would be a good one! Others might include: "all mine," "nothing gets past me," or a mechanical reminder such as "stay down."

- **Pound your fist into your glove once or twice,** tap the back of your glove against your thigh, or shift your weight from one foot to the other to trigger your concentration.

Any of these ideas can be combined into a simple routine. For example, you might want to have your routine be to tap your fist into your glove twice as you think "hit it to me" and step into your circle.

For catchers, you may want to have a routine that you take a breath after you throw the ball back to the pitcher (for control), decide on and signal the next pitch (plan), and use your glove going up to the target as your cue to shift into trust mode. You may want to use a word or short phrase to help click in your concentration such as "soft" or "stay loose." Also, nodding your head to the pitcher as you set up the target tells the pitcher that you are with him and this is the right pitch.

Here are a couple more examples of players working through the self-control, plan, trust process:

Infielder
Self-Control: Take a breath.

Plan: Leadoff hitter, nobody on or out, he runs well. "See the ball and react."

Trust: Step into the circle of focus.

Outfielder
Self-control: Checks in and recognizes that he really wasn't focused on that last pitch. "Hey, let's go," he says to himself as he bounces up and down a couple of times to get some blood flowing.

Plan: Man on first base, two outs. Yells to his centerfielder "Two outs, no doubles here" and visualizes a fly ball being hit his way.

Trust: Steps into his circle of focus and thinks "hit it to me" as the pitcher starts his delivery.

Release: What to Do When You Make an Error

Once you have a routine, you now need a plan for handling your yellow and red lights on defense. In particular, have a strategy to release the emotions that usually come with an error.

Errors are part of the game. We don't want you to spend a lot of time thinking about making errors, but we do want you to be prepared to handle them. Having a plan for dealing with errors is not negative thinking, it's thinking ahead.

Your release doesn't have to be reserved for times when you make an error. You may need to use it more frequently to let go of an at bat that you are upset about. **IT'S CRITICAL TO BE ABLE TO SEPARATE OFFENSE AND DEFENSE.** If you go back to the field thinking about your last at bat you will at least get a bad jump on a ball hit to you, and there's a good chance you'll misplay the ball. Your release is something you can use to help leave your bat in the dugout and focus on playing defense.

Keep this in mind: college coaches and pro scouts often hope players they scout make an error or face some other adversity so they can see how the player handles it. Can he overcome adversity or does he lose control when he makes one mistake or has a bad at bat? The answer often determines whether or not a player is recruited or drafted.

Errors are often the result of batters bringing their at bats with them to the field.

Here are some suggestions for developing your own "release:"

- Take a breath. Chances are your face, neck and chest muscles are tight with anger and frustration. Take a couple of breaths and make sure your muscles let go as you exhale.

- Use your focal point. It tells you that you're fine, you've worked hard, you deserve to trust yourself and that you should just focus on the next pitch.

- Take off your glove or hat. While the hat or glove is off you can be disgusted. When you put it back on, however, it means you are ready to focus on the next pitch.

- Turn your back to the plate. You can be upset when your back is to the plate; when you turn around everything is positive and focused on determining your plan for this next pitch. Use this one when you need to "turn it around" defensively.

- Smooth things over. Wipe smooth a footprint in the dirt with your foot to clear away the last play or your last at bat.

- Pick up some grass or a rock, or anything else handy. Squeeze the object and put all your negative emotions into it. When you're ready, throw the object and your negatives away.

- Lift your sternum into a confident position. You're probably hanging your head pretty low. Make a conscious effort to raise it up and carry yourself the way a great fielder would.

- Talk to your teammates between pitches. Players often get "internal" when they're down and go to war with themselves. Use the time between pitches to check in on yourself, but get your focus and energy going out in order to play well during the pitches. Talk over positioning, fly ball responsibilities, coverages, or anything else you can think of to get your energy going out onto the game.

You may want to combine two or more of these ideas. For example, turn your back to the plate, take a couple of deep breaths and look to your focal point to release your error.

Play with these ideas in your next practice and get clear on what your strategy will be for releasing an error or a frustrating at bat.

The series of photos on the following page shows a player working the process of releasing an error. After the ball goes through his legs **(1),** the angered fielder turns his back to the plate, takes off his hat and takes a quality

1   2   3

breath **(2)**. After a few moments, he lifts his head, puts on his hat and turns confidently toward home plate **(3)**. Just before the next pitch he steps into his circle of focus and thinks, "Hit it to me." This process doesn't guarantee that he will be focused and ready for the next pitch, but it does give him something to go to when he needs it most.

Pregame Preparation

The general concepts of pregame preparation were discussed in Chapter 5. We discussed such things as having a definite time that you become a ballplayer, getting yourself in the mood to play and familiarizing yourself with the field conditions where you will be playing.

Preparation for playing defense begins with getting your body ready to play. Run, stretch, throw and do whatever else you need to do to get ready. It's important to get your body ready before you throw or take fungoes because it lessens your chances of injury and makes it more likely you'll get a good start fielding balls. Successfully fielding balls at the beginning of batting practice builds confidence you can carry into the game. If you aren't ready to start fielding baseballs, you're more likely not to make plays you know you can make, setting the stage for the spiral of frustration to begin.

You may want to do a few drills to remind you of your good fielding mechanics. A few minutes of "maintenance" work on your mechanics each day keeps you from drifting into bad habits. When fielding mechanics become faulty it's usually a gradual process rather than something that happens over-night. Do drills you used during your preseason training sessions to keep your mechanics sharp.

Finally, you are prepared to take balls off a bat in the infield or outfield. Your approach is what is most important. If you want your efforts in prac-tice to help you in a game, make the fungoes and balls off the bat in batting practice as game-like as possible. That is, focus on them just as you will focus on balls hit to you during the game.

A good way to think of this is to respect each ball hit to you. If you respect each fungo you will focus on the ball and use your good mechanics. You are much better off taking 10 quality fungoes than taking 50 if you are just going through the motions.

This is the difference between practicing your defensive skills and "shag-ging balls." Occasionally, you'll want to take a break to relax and shag balls. That's OK because your relaxing has a purpose — to get you ready for your next focused practice session.

Taking Infield/Outfield

Like the bullpen for pitchers and batting practice for hitters, pregame in-field or outfield is important. It often sets the tone for the game and serves as the punctuation mark on the end of the pregame preparations. Although in-field is important, players often put too much emphasis on how it goes, on the "outcome" of infield. Instead of treating it simply as part of the process of getting ready to play a game, they let infield determine their confidence going into a game — if they have a good infield they'll play well, if they have a poor infield they'll play badly.

Preparation is the key to having a good infield. When you (and your teammates) are mentally prepared to take infield, you are focused and ener-gized, and the ball is thrown crisply. When you aren't prepared — whether you aren't physically warmed up or are mentally somewhere else — there are lots of bad hops and balls get thrown all over the place. Frustration and embarrassment begin to escalate with each miscue, and players come off the field angry and filled with doubts about their ability to perform that day.

Prepare yourself by working your body to get it ready. Take a few mo-ments to visualize yourself having a good infield and doing the things that you are capable of doing. If you focus on trying to impress the other team or the scouts rather than on the ingredients of playing the game, you set yourself up for difficulty.

Baserunning: A "Next Base" Mentality

Heads-up baserunning wins games. Many games are decided because an alert base runner took one extra base which led to one extra run which meant the difference between winning or losing.

> Baserunning isn't just about speed. Speed is great if you have it, but if you don't have quickness in your legs you can still be an excellent base runner by being quick with your mind. Taking an aggressive lead to distract the pitcher, faking a steal and getting a good jump on a base hit are some things you can do to get an advantage on the other team regardless of what kind of "wheels" you have. Good baserunning is as much about having the right mind-set as it is about having physical tools.

A big part of that right mind-set is thinking "next base." Good base runners aren't satisfied with getting a hit; their mission is to score a run. Whether it's going from first to third on a single, scoring from first on a double, or moving from second to third when the ball rolls away from the catcher, they're always looking for a way to take that "extra" base.

You want to be aggressive on the base paths, but you also can't afford to give away outs. Be smart about getting to the "next base" by taking baserunning one pitch at a time. Here's how the **self-control, plan, trust** model applies to base running.

On the Base: Self-Control

The first step to running bases one pitch at a time is to be under control. When you're under control you are able to anticipate what might happen on the next pitch and your mind is clear to make the split-second decisions necessary on the base paths.

When you aren't under control you are tight both mentally and physically resulting in bad jumps on batted balls and bad decisions about at which base to stop. Some runners get so out of control they forget to look to the third base coach for the signs before the pitch or as they approach second base on a base hit! If you can't remember to look to your coach for signs, you aren't in control of yourself.

> The key to being in control during a pitch is to be in control **before** the pitch is thrown. Although it's usually good to be on base, baserunners often are upset about their at bats. Maybe they swung at a bad pitch but looped it for a hit or reached on an error, or they walked but wanted a chance to hit, or maybe they don't respect the importance of baserunning so they space out a bit. On the other hand, don't get so excited about what you did at the plate that you fail to focus on what you're doing now, as when George Brett was picked off first base after knocking his 3,000th hit!

Get into the habit of checking in on your traffic light when you reach base. Am I in control? Am I focused on this pitch? Am I thinking "next base?"

Here are a some ideas you can use if you find that you aren't quite in control of yourself when you are on base:

- **Take a breath.** It will help you get your focus on the present moment and clear your head.

- **Go to your focal point.** It can tell you that you're OK, you're on base now, so just do a good job.

- **Use a "release."** Let go of your unproductive thoughts by using the release you use when you are on defense or hitting, or come up with one for when you're on base. For example, taking off your batting gloves could mean you are done hitting and are now focused on putting pressure on the other team.

- **Talk to yourself.** Go through a couple of possibilities such as what you'll do on a ground ball to the shortstop or a fly ball to the outfield, or go over the situation with your base coach.

On the Base: Plan

A player's instincts for the game play a critical role in baserunning. Although instincts are largely natural, they can be improved. The first issue here is experience. The more time you've spent on base in a game situation, the better you are at reacting to what happens.

Secondly, as is the case when you are playing defense, the more you've anticipated different scenarios, the more likely you are to make quick, correct decisions when the heat is on.

The first step of anticipation is to examine the situation. Things to consider include the signals from your coach, the number of outs, the score, positioning of the infielders and outfielders, the catcher's arm strength and field conditions.

Just as in fielding, visualize a few possibilities. Visualize the hitter singling sharply to right or a ground ball being hit to the shortstop. Your base coaches are helping you with this by saying "halfway on a fly ball," or "you've gotta go on a ground ball" and things like that, but don't just rely on them; think through some possibilities on your own.

It only takes an instant — probably less than 5 seconds — to think of these possibilities. Nonetheless, you still can't anticipate everything that could happen. But thinking one or two things that might happen and scheming about ways to get to the next base put you in the frame of mind you need to be in just before each pitch.

*Roberto Alomar steals another base. While standing on the base, make sure you're under **CONTROL** and have a **PLAN**. Once you take your lead, you don't have time to think. You simply focus on the pitcher and **TRUST** your reactions.*

As You Get Off the Base: Trust

Your self-control and planning are done when you are standing on the base and can afford to not be fully focused on the baseball. Stepping off the base to take your lead, however, is your cue to switch into your trust mode. Your focus has got to be on a spot or area on the pitcher. If you are off the base and not locked in on the pitcher you are leaving the door open for trouble.

The planning you do before the pitch puts your mind in position to simply react to what you see — there's no time to ponder what you should do when the ball is hit or gets away from the catcher. For example, a lot of coaches are now teaching their base runners, particularly when they are on first base, to watch the pitch on its way to home plate. If they read that the ball is going to be in the dirt they are to either take off for the next base or at least extend their secondary lead. There's no time for thinking, you either go or stay. You have to trust your judgment.

The Coach's Box

Players are often not in control of themselves enough during a game to remember to take a breath. Whether they are on base, in the field, or at the plate, emotions can cloud their thinking. Develop a way to remind players from the dugout or coach's box when it's a good time to take a breath. A simple suggestion is to pat yourself on your stomach like you just ate a big meal.

The breath can also help keep your thinking clear during a game. You need to be planning for later innings and helping your players make adjustments over the course of a game, so you can't afford to either get caught up in the excitement of a late inning rally or let your mind drift away from the game. Take a breath at the start of every inning as a way to check in to make sure you are in control and are focused on the game.

How to Work on Your Mental Game in Practice

How can I improve my reactions to the pressures of the late innings in a close game? How can I get out of a slump? What can I do to gain more confidence? How can I become more consistent?

Players often ask these questions about the mental game. Since everything we've talked about so far can be applied to these problems, at this point you should have some good ideas on how to solve them. The content of our responses to these questions is found in previous chapters, but the place where all of these ideas come together is practice.

Practice is where the action is. How you react in clutch situations or how much confidence you have isn't determined when the moment arrives -- it's determined by the way you prepare for that moment in your preseason and daily workouts.

> Specifically, the quality of your practices determines your reactions to pressure situations. A quality practice involves doing things with the same intensity and focus you use in a game. Thus, the main theme for this chapter is that you need to **PRACTICE WHAT YOU ARE GOING TO DO IN A GAME.**

Trying to do things in a game that you haven't practiced is not the situation you want to be in. Since you will have to deal with adversity in a game, work on it in practice. Similarly, work on trusting yourself and "freeing it up" in practice just as you will need to do in a game. It's great if your coach helps you with these things, but don't expect him to do it for you. **The quality of your practices is your responsibility.**

All of the ideas we've talked about — from taking a breath to using your focal point to visualization — can easily be worked into your practices (and need to be if you want them to help you in your games). We'll give you some specific ways to do that, but keep these two basic ideas in mind:

1) **Have a purpose or mission.** In other words, know what you are trying to accomplish. Just as hitters often "give away" at bats because they aren't focused on each pitch, players often "give away" practice time because they are just going through the motions. Don't go into a bullpen or batting practice to just "see what happens." Take control of the situation by having a simple but definite plan for what you are trying to do.

2) **Have a present moment focus.** The idea of "one pitch at a time" becomes one drill repetition, one sprint, or one whatever at a time in practice. Since you need to focus on the present moment in a game, practice it in practice. In short, **make practice like a game so that in a game you can make it "just like practice."** That kind of quality practice builds confidence.

Because coaches often search for ways to work on the mental game in practice, suggestions for how a team or individual could implement these ideas are included.

Mental Preparation for Practice

Good preparation greatly enhances your chances of having a quality practice. The ideas for preparation from Chapter 5 can be applied when preparing for a practice as well. Here are a few reminders:

- **Look forward to practice.** Spend a little time during the day thinking about practice. Visualize yourself working on a part of your game that has been giving you trouble or that you are trying to improve. Don't get into anything really involved, just see yourself doing a few things well and see if you can get yourself to look forward to practice. If dreading practice is a frequent feeling for you, check in on your mission (Chapter 2) in baseball.

- **Pick a time when practice starts.** Set a moment — getting into your car to go to practice, changing your clothes or lining up for your team stretch — that you become a ballplayer. Leave your off-the-field concerns off the field and focus on baseball. Don't worry, they will be there when practice is over.

- **Set a mission or two for the day.** This is the most important part of your practice preparation. Look back at your answers to the questions about your mission in baseball in Chapter 2. If, for example, you want to be known as a hard worker or look back on your career and say you got the most of your ability, you need to do those things **TODAY.**

The mission could be mechanical, such as improving your follow through, or mental, such as taking pride in everything you do during the practice. You may have two or three missions on a given day, but more than that gets cumbersome.

Coaches, letting your players know the practice schedule for the day and reminding them about the importance of having a mission is a big help. Have your players write down a mission or two at the start of practice on occasion. This gets them into the habit and gives you an idea what they are working on.

Going Through the Motions

Once practice begins, you need to recognize the difference between putting in quality, focused practice and just going through the motions. The following exercise will enhance your understanding.

1) Lift your right arm up and down five times as fast as you can as if you are a bird trying to take off.

2) Take your right arm and move it up and down just one time, **BUT DO IT VERY SLOWLY.** Close your eyes and focus on the feelings involved in raising and lowering your arm. Notice the sensation of the air moving against your hand. Does the air change temperature along the way? Feel the muscles in your shoulder get tense as you lift your arm. Feel the muscles in your rib cage as you stretch your arm up way over your head. Notice the same things in reverse on the way down.

What differences did you notice between the two? Both involved "raising and lowering your arm," but you should have found them to be quite different.

In the first case you were simply "going through the motions." You just pumped the arm and probably had few sensations involved in doing it. In the second case, however, you had more awareness of what was going on. The same muscles were used, but you had a fuller, richer experience and learned much more about what is involved in raising your arm the second way. You "paid attention" in the second case.

Quality practice is paying attention. It involves doing things with a purpose and in having your mind fully engaged in what you are doing **right now.**

Quality Work in Action

> The focus you used in the arm raising exercise can be used in anything you do in practice. You don't need to change your practice routine to have a quality practice. The only change you need to make is approaching your practice with a greater sense of purpose.

Here are a few examples:

Focused Stretch. Instead of yapping with your buddies while you stretch, take a few moments to put in some quality stretching. Use your breath as you stretch; relax as you exhale and let yourself go deeper into the stretch. Focusing on the muscle being stretched gives you a good opportunity to feel the effects of a good breath.

Use the team stretch at the start of each practice to "check in" on how your body is feeling and to make use of your breath. It's also a good time to set your mission(s) for the day.

Focused Catch. Instead of just "getting loose" or "playing catch," play focused catch. Pick out a particular target — right shoulder, head, left knee — on your partner, and throw to that point. Your goal isn't just to hit your partner, it's to hit a particular spot on your partner. This gives each throw a "mini-

"I hate to see guys play catch and just throw the ball back and forth. There's no feedback, there's no goal. Every time you throw the ball in a game you're going to have some place you're trying to throw it, so you'd better do the same thing in practice."
— Marcel Lachemann, California Angels manager

mission." It doesn't mean you "try hard" and aim the ball, but instead your focus connects you with the target and you let the ball go. This is how you'll throw in a game so do it in practice.

Augie Garrido, coach of two national championship teams at Cal-State Fullerton, uses focused catch as a way of telling who is clicked in to what he is doing and who isn't. If players are chasing balls or talking and not hitting spots, it's pretty clear they aren't where they need to be. Focused catch (or any other drill) can become a way of taking "mental attendance" at practice.

Simulation. Top performers in all areas — from astronauts to surgeons to Olympians — make extensive use of simulation to enhance the quality of their practice. The idea is to make practice as much like a game as possible, and it's largely a matter of being a little creative.

For example, have players running from home to first when fungoes are hit to the infielders. Similarly, live baserunners add intensity as you work on cutoffs and relays with the outfielders. If a fielder makes an error, make sure he goes through his "release" before hitting him another one.

Relaxation and Imagery. A great way to develop concentration and self-control in practice is by taking five to 20 minutes and going through a relaxation and imagery session. (Details on this can be found in the Appendix.) Coach, taking time to do this during regular practice time tells your players that you think the mental game is important.

Turning It Around in Practice

Anyone can practice well when he feels like practicing. But heads-up players turn it around and get in some quality time even when they don't feel like practicing or when practice is going poorly. Players who get the most from their ability don't necessarily feel like practicing more often than other players, the commitment to their mission pushes them to put in quality work regardless of how they feel.

The first step in turning it around is recognizing when you aren't putting in quality work (like pumping your arm up and down mindlessly). Get into the habit of checking in on yourself in practice. Ask yourself if you have a purpose for what you are doing and if your mind is fully engaged on what you are doing. Coaches can help a great deal with this by simply stopping practice and asking players to evaluate or grade themselves on the quality of their practice to that point.

Here are some ideas you can use to turn it around if you find you aren't where you need to be mentally:

The 2-Minute Drill. For two minutes see how well you can practice. Just two minutes. You can do it for that long no matter how you feel. Don't go wild like a football defensive lineman, but click in to your best quality, focused effort. Make it like a two-minute slice of your best practice ever, or pretend a pro scout just showed up to check you out.

After two minutes or so (hopefully you don't have a watch on), stop and ask yourself, "What did I do to click it in?" "What did I focus on?" "What did I say to myself?" "What did I do with my body?" The answers to these questions are important because they tell you what you need to do to get yourself going. Not only can this information enhance the quality of your practices, it also tells you what to do when you need to turn it around in a game.

Coaches can effectively use the two-minute drill any time they feel practice isn't going as well as it could. Once the team knows the drill, yell that you're going into a two-minute drill. After two minutes call the team together and ask the players what they did to get themselves focused. Their responses provide information you can remind them of in pressure situations.

Use Your Releases. Throughout the book we've talked about having a way to let go of "yellow- and red-light" events such as giving up a home run, making an error and swinging at a bad pitch. Reading this book doesn't mean you'll be able to do the stuff that's in it. **Don't expect your strategies for releasing negative emotions to be very effective if you don't practice them.** Would you expect to turn many double plays in a game if you never worked on them?

Make sure, for example, that you have a **focal point** to go to when you have a bad round of batting practice, when you let a ball roll through your legs, when you can't throw a curveball more than 58 feet in the bullpen, or when your coach says something that gets under your skin.

Also, work on your deep **breaths.** The more you work with it, the more the breath will help you.

In the next three sections we'll cover specific examples of how to work on your mental skills in the four different phases of the game.

Pitching

> **Have a mission for your bullpen.** Whether it's in preseason or between appearances, be proactive. You dictate what goes on in the pen rather than letting the bullpen decide for you.

Without a mission, you can easily end up looking for things to go wrong instead of working on something you need to work on. You may bounce a couple of curveballs, get upset, and spend the rest of the bullpen cranking curveballs even though your curveball was good in the last outing.

Here are some examples of bullpen missions:

"I'm going to —

- *work on my rhythm and my change-up."*
- *work on staying free and easy."*
- *work on staying back."*
- *work on pitching from the stretch."*
- *work on my routine and my release."*
- *find a key word or phrase to tell me what I need to do on each pitch."*

You will certainly work on some things other than those specified in your mission, but your mission will be the centerpiece of your "side piece." Walking away from your bullpen having accomplished a mission rather than simply "throwing a pen" should be your goal.

Work on your routine. Your routine isn't just something you use in a game. It's your best friend when you're out there doing battle; work on it the same way you would work on your curveball or slider. You've got to be able to stick with it when the winning run is on second base. There's no better place to work on it in than the stress-free environment of practice.

Play with your routine a little; try some different things. It's generally best that your routine doesn't involve doing something radically different from what you usually do anyway. The difference will be that now your actions between pitches will have a purpose instead of being a mindless habit.

Remember, get your self under control, get clear on your plan for the pitch, then trust it.

Take a Breath Before Each Pitch. This should already be part of your routine, but we wanted to emphasize it here. Work with it in practice for a few days and see if it doesn't help you feel more controlled (which can help you stay back longer, for example), and help you establish a sense of rhythm to your pitching. Remember, it's a pretty easy thing to do in practice, but it's tough when the pressure is on in a game.

You may find that you prefer not to use it when you are throwing well, but keep practicing it so it's there to go to when you need it.

Work on Your Release. You will have adversity in a game, so practice dealing with it. In the bullpen, when you feel a little frustrated and a yellow light is coming on, use your release to let it go and get yourself back to that centered and balanced feeling.

Shadow It. Shadow pitching is going through the motions of pitching without a ball. Instead of using a ball, visualize the pitch going to a catcher. This is one of the best mental game drills there is. You can use it everyday because it doesn't strain your arm, you can simulate anything that might happen in a game, and it isn't something new or unusual. In fact, you may use shadow pitching — sometimes called "dry mechanics" — to work on your delivery already.

You can now use shadow pitching to:

1) **Work on Your Routine.** The series of photos on page 92 in Chapter 6, demonstrates a pitcher working on his routine using shadow pitching.

2) **Find Your Rhythm and Build Your Confidence.** Visualize yourself pitching great and mowing down batters. Go back to your best outing and "reenact" a few innings of it, getting a sense of the rhythm you have when you're pitching great. As you know, pitching great, even if it is mostly in your mind, is a big boost to your confidence.

3) **Practice Dealing with Adversity.** Now that things are going well, visualize yourself hitting some yellow and red lights. Shadow a pitch and pretend that you just went 2-0 on a batter, that you gave up a bloop hit on a good pitch, that your shortstop booted a routine ground ball, that you walked a guy, that you gave up a home run (a really long one — the kind that should almost count for two runs), or that you made a great pitch but got squeezed by the umpire. Go through your release, it may be just an extra breath before you step on or it may be a walk behind the mound, and then come back and make a good pitch. The more you get into it, the more effective it will be for you.

DON'T WORRY if you can't "see" your pitch, your catcher, a batter or anything else. A lot of people can't. Visualizing is a skill that you'll get better at with time. In the meantime, just think of pretending all these things are happening the way you pretended to be pitching in the World Series when you were a kid.

Long Beach State pitcher Mike Fontana pitches in a College World Series game in Omaha. (Long Beach State photo)

Coaches, you probably already use shadow pitching for working on mechanics. Now take the extra step and use it on the mental game. You can work with individuals, pairs or the whole staff at once. Have them shadow pitch throwing well for a couple of minutes — again looking to establish a sense of rhythm — then have them shadow dealing with adversity.

You can use shadow pitching to introduce the whole idea of using a routine. Start by telling your pitchers to take a slow, steady breath before each pitch. Line them up using a foul line or a line in the gym as the rubber and have them go through their full windup, including taking the sign from the catcher. Make sure they take a breath before each pitch. Tell them to experiment when they take the breath. Some may like to take it just after they step on the rubber, some just after they get the sign and some just as they start their motion. Encourage them to try to "see" the pitch they threw hit the catcher's mitt. After each pitch they should pretend to get the ball back and start this one breath routine over again.

> *"The key was having spent so much time shadow pitching and dealing with adversity. I knew there'd be times when I'd disagree with the ump on balls and strikes, and I knew there would be thousands of screaming fans, but I handled it well because I had prepared for it all season."*
> *— Long Beach State pitcher Mike Fontana on winning two College World Series games*

Next, explain the idea of using a release and some possible options (wiping the dirt off the rubber, taking an extra breath before they step on the rubber, taking off their glove, etc.) Have them shadow a pitch they knew was a strike but was called a ball. Watch them go through a release of some type, get back on the rubber, take their breath and throw the next pitch.

Another highly effective variation is to have a coach or another player stand behind the player who is shadow pitching and have the coach tell the pitcher the outcome of his pitch. For example, have the pitcher go through his delivery and you say "Ball one." On the next pitch, "Ball two" and so forth. Make it tough on the pitcher by introducing distractions, including teammates razzing the pitcher. See if he can stick to his routine and use his release.

It may take a few times to get comfortable with it, but keep emphasizing that their ability to establish a rhythm, release negatives and pitch the game one pitch at a time is what will determine how well they pitch, so they'd better practice doing it.

Hitting

Have a Mission for Batting Practice. A batting practice mission is just like the "plan" we talked about in the hitting chapter. Decide on a purpose for what you will be trying to do at the plate **before** you get into the cage.

Thinking through your mission also helps mentally prepare you for your round in the batting cage. Mindlessly going in to "see what happens" or, worse, going in to play Home Run Derby is almost asking for bad things to happen. Hitters often step in without being ready. After a couple of pop-ups they get upset and storm out of the cage, probably blaming it on the guy throwing batting practice.

> Don't leave what happens in batting practice to chance. Go in with a mission like "stay back," "hit it back up the middle," "hit it where it is pitched," "trust my swing," "pivot on my back side," "keep my head down," or even "just see it and hit it." You then evaluate your round based on how well you did on your mission, not on how many balls you hit into the seats.

Work on Your Routine. If your routine is going to help you in a game, it must be practiced. For example, if putting on your helmet is the start of your at bat, use it as the start of your batting practice. Don't mindlessly put it on; make it a meaningful event that helps you mentally prepare for what you are about to do. Intrasquad scrimmages are a great time to work on your routine, but you can also use your routine at the plate during your drills in practice.

Coaches, you may want to have a hitting station where the batter goes through his routine before each pitch just as he will in a game. Batters also can practice their routine when standing at the plate taking pitches in the bullpen or during indoor practices.

"When I think about times or at bats that have been successful, I try to envision even the sounds and smells and feelings that I had."
— Paul Molitor, Toronto Blue Jays

Take a Breath Between Pitches. See if you can get yourself to take a breath at some point before each swing you take in practice. That includes your soft toss drills, your cuts off a pitching machine, and your shadow or dry swings. It sounds simple but requires a lot of discipline. The breath helps release your previous swing and gets you focused for the next one. In short, it raises the quality of your practice.

At the Long Beach State hitting camp, players learn to take a good breath and work it into their routine, then spend an entire day using the breathing routine before each swing they take in a drill. Head Coach Dave Snow says the difference is apparent. "The quality of their focus throughout the day is much better when we have them take a breath before each pitch or each swing than if we let them just hack away," says Snow.

Coaches, try making a rule in batting practice that the ball is not thrown until the batter takes a breath. It won't slow batting practice down as much as you think, and it helps the batters focus. To introduce the idea, have one "deep-breath round" where each batter takes a breath before each pitch. It may not be love at first sight for your hitters, but stick with it for at least a week and see if they come to recognize how much it helps them.

Practice Regrouping at the Plate. Getting yourself back together after something negative happens at the plate is one of the most important skills you can have. Mentally tough batters can swing and miss at a bad pitch, have a bad call go against them, or barely avoid being decapitated by a pitch and still get themselves back to being centered and balanced for the next pitch. The more you practice this, the better you'll be at it.

Anytime, be it in a round of batting practice or during drills, that you feel any emotion that you don't want, step back and use your release.

Coaches, when one of your players starts to struggle during a round of batting practice, give him a moment to step out of the box, take a breath, go to his focal point and step back in. Remember, the quality of practice is more important than the quantity. Also, a hitting station to practice releasing and regrouping at the plate could be part of your drill work. For example, have a batter intentionally miss a pitch that is way low in soft toss or short toss drills, go through his release, and then hit the next toss.

Shadow It. In shadow hitting, sometimes called "dry swings," you use your regular bat and imagine yourself facing pitches thrown to you. Like shadow pitching, shadow hitting is a great way to work on all of the mental aspects of hitting. Here are a few ways you can use it:

1) Visualize pitches coming to different parts of the strike zone and hitting them to the appropriate fields (pull the inside ones, hit the ones down the middle up the middle, drive the outside ones to the opposite field). See how well you can visualize the ball coming out of a pitcher's release point. Shadow at least 20 pitches a day.

2) Gain confidence by "reenacting" your best at bats ever. Go back in time to a game when you were on fire; see how clearly you can see those pitches coming in and how close you can get to generating the feeling that you had. This can be a good confidence booster and slump breaker.

3) Reenact one of your worst at bats, but don't dwell on it. Instead, repeat the at bat using your routine and your release to get regrouped before the pitch that got you out. This time, see yourself either laying off the pitch or driving it for a base hit.

Coaches, you can use shadow hitting to introduce the idea of routines and releases to your hitters. The minutes leading up to an at bat are often what decide the success of the at bat, but few coaches teach their hitters what to do during that time. Gather your hitters around you while you go through a sample routine starting from the time you leave the dugout. Explain to them what you are doing at each point by saying out loud the things you would be saying to yourself. Take it all the way through the at bat (include swinging at a bad pitch or something so that you have to use your release) so they can get a feel for the whole process.

Remind them that you are giving them some ideas and that it is important for each player to develop his own routine.

Fielding

Have a Mission in Mind. By this point, you might be tired of reading about having a mission, but a sense of purpose and direction adds quality to what you are doing and is a source of satisfaction when you accomplish what you set out to do.

> Your mission might simply be to have fun. The rest of the mental game tends to take care of itself when you are having fun. Other possible missions might be to work on balls to your left, to stay loose, to play each ball as if you are playing a game, to work on your routine, or to work on coming back after making an error.

Work on Your Routine. The best way to enhance your fielding skills is through quality work in practice. Use your routine to channel your focus down to where you are confident and playing one pitch (or fungo) at a time. Thus, a great way to enhance your skills as a fielder is to work with your routine in practice.

If your prepitch routine is to tap the back of your glove against your thigh, step into your circle of focus and think "Hit it to me," do that in practice. Step into your **CIRCLE OF FOCUS** before a fungo is hit to you.

Work on Your Release. Use making an error in practice an opportunity to go to your focal point, take a breath, turn your back to the plate for a moment, or whatever you use for your release. Making the effort not only better enables you to let go of an error or a bad at bat, but also helps you keep from spiraling out of control in practice.

A good defensive drill is to practice making errors. In the drill, the fielder intentionally boots a ball (or shadows it), goes through his release, then successfully makes the play on the next fungo. (Repeat as needed!) Then the next player steps forward for his turn.

Use Your Focal Point. Your focal point is particularly important on defense because it's easy to lose your focus — your mind has a lot of time to wander among many distractions. Using your focal point in practice helps you develop the habit of going to it to release negative thoughts and emotions or to regain your focus. When your mind wanders from being focused and confident, use your focal point to catch it, bring it back and remind you of your mission.

Shadow It. Fielding without using a ball is a great way to work on your mental game as well as your mechanics. Practice your routine (for when you have a green light) and your release (for when you have a yellow or red light). A whole team can work on its routines and releases together.

Coaches, put each player at his position and have him shadow his routines as a pitcher shadows making a pitch. Call out the result of the pitch — a ball or a strike — and watch for the fielders to stand up and step back from their circles. On the next pitch tell them to imagine that they made an error and watch everyone on the field go through his release.

In order to help your players separate offense and defense, start the drill with the whole team in the dugout. Tell them to imagine that they just struck out with the bases loaded to end the sixth inning in a tie ball game and they are not happy about it. Have them show you how they will release that at bat and focus on defense as they warm up for next inning.

What goes on between pitches largely determines what goes on during them, so invest a little time practicing using that time effectively.

> Maintain the quality of your shadow work. Don't just "go through the motions" because you are just going through the motions!

Baserunning

Run the bases in practice with the level of **focus** and **respect** you use in a game. The good instincts and anticipation we talked about in the last chapter as being so important to baserunning are developed through experience — game or game-like intensity experience, that is. Strolling around the bases halfheartedly during batting practice doesn't count as experience nor does it improve your baserunning skills.

Get excited about baserunning; work on getting a good lead and reading the ball off the bat. Also, set yourself apart — coaches like to see guys who care about getting better.

End-of-Practice Evaluation

It's important to spend a brief amount of time at the end of practice or later that day evaluating what you did. First, how did you do with your mission(s)? If you accomplished your mission, how did you do it? If you didn't accomplish it, what is the explanation for that?

You can also review what your coach taught you that day, or remind yourself of something you figured out on your own such as what you did during a two-minute drill or a change you made on your routine. Again, although it takes considerable discipline, a journal is a great tool for maximizing your learning.

The bottom line to practice is learning. What did you learn today?

The Mental Game in the Weight Room

Not all of your efforts to improve yourself take place on the field. In fact, many players make greater gains in the off-season than they do during the season. The weight room is one area where these gains are made. Here are some ideas that can help you get the most out of your time in the weight room while working on your mental game at the same time.

Have a Mission. Your mission for your career in baseball should inspire your efforts in your off-season as well as your in-season workouts. In other words, your mission should help you get into the weight room.

Once you're there, have your workouts designed so that you know what you want to accomplish when you walk in the room. The players who get the most out of their time in the weight room are the ones who have a sense of being on a mission.

Take It One Repetition at a Time. Keep a full focus on each rep. Your focus is a major source of strength. If you lose your focus during a set, you're bound to lose some strength. Specifically, most trainers recommend that you **keep your mind in the muscle you are working.** This focus enhances the quality of your repetitions. The better the quality of your reps, the more benefits you get from them.

Use Your Breath. The weight room is a great place to work with your breathing. You can use your breath before a set to psych yourself up or to relax muscles you are about to use.

Regardless of the exercise you are doing, basic weight training technique calls for you to exhale as the weight is being lifted and inhale as the weight is coming down. Not only does this help you physiologically, but psychologically it helps you keep your focus and relax muscles that should be relaxed during the exercise. For example, a lot of players will tense their neck muscles when doing the bench press. Use your breath to relax your neck while your chest and triceps are working hard.

Stretching. In order to maintain or increase the all-important flexibility of your muscles, make sure you do a great job of stretching your muscles both before and after you lift. **Be sure to talk with your coach before beginning any weight training program.**

Special Opportunities to Learn

10

The best players in baseball constantly seek ways to learn and relentlessly pursue information that might improve their performance. Many of them claim this quest is an important factor in their success. Lessons can be drawn from any experience, but some are particularly instructive.

This chapter examines four such experiences. The first three, ***Dealing with Failing and Losing, Succeeding as a Role Player*** and ***Coming Back from Injury*** deal with some of the most emotionally difficult situations in baseball. Seeing them as opportunities to learn makes them less unpleasant and also assists in overcoming them. In each case, keep in mind that the mental game is like the weight room: you get stronger by pushing heavier weights. The final section explores how using the ideas in this book and your own baseball experiences enhance your performance in ***Life Outside of Baseball.***

Dealing with Failing and Losing

You will experience failure. Baseball is a game of failure; the only way to avoid it is to not play. Even the best players make outs, boot ground balls, walk in winning runs, drop game-losing fly balls, strike out with the bases loaded, slump for two weeks and have bad seasons. The question isn't whether you will face adversity but how will you respond to it. There is no value in dwelling on failure but it must be recognized as part of the game. We don't see this as negative thinking, we see it as facing reality.

Your natural talent and hard work allow you to succeed as you climb the baseball ladder from youth leagues to high school to college and, for some, to the professional level. At some point, though, you will need the mental skills explained in this book. It happens to everybody, so don't be surprised by it.

It's OK to Feel Down

It's natural to feel upset when you perform poorly or to feel a sense of loss when your team is beaten. You can be upset, dejected or sad for a little while, so give yourself permission to feel that way. A great thing about being human is the wide range of emotions we experience; experiencing failure and loss can help make you *more* human (which we see as a positive). Of course, it's not OK to do anything damaging to yourself, anyone else or anything of value, and we recommend putting off any major decisions until you get over these feelings.

> *"There's too much at stake to spend time being upset. You must develop the ability to learn from what just happened, then forgive yourself for doing it. Learn and forgive: Once you've done that, you've done all you can do."*
> — **Dr. Curt Tribble,**
> **heart surgeon**

To help you move through your "down time," set a time limit for yourself to let go of the negative emotions, learn from the experience and get on with life. Give yourself an hour, three hours, overnight or 24 hours, then shift your focus. There's no benefit to "spiraling out of control" with negative thoughts for days.

If you think moping around for days shows your commitment and how much you care, think again. Are you committed to playing your best baseball or to demonstrating that you care about your loss or mistake? When your goal is to play your best and enjoy your time in baseball, learn from the experience then shift your focus from the failure to your next task.

Define Failure Intelligently

How do you know when you fail? How do you know when you succeed? Your answers reveal your perspective on the game. Throughout this book, the idea that you need to focus on things over which you have control instead of concerns outside of your control has been emphasized again and again. If your answers to our questions mention things outside of your control, such as losing, getting hits or getting batters out, reconsider your thinking. Basing your feelings of success and failure on things outside of your control sets you up for the roller coaster ride we spoke of in Chapter 3.

Feeling badly about a loss or a slump is OK, but don't let these temporary shortfalls define you as a failure. Feeling dejected because you lost is one thing, labeling it a failure is destructive. Make a clear distinction between your performance and your feelings about yourself as a person. Although your performance did not allow you to get the outcome you were hoping for, your value as a person is not diminished because of it. Even if your performance was terrible, it doesn't make you a terrible person. As obvious as this sounds, players often fail to distinguish themselves from their performances.

Evaluate your performance on things that are within your control. Were you focused on the process of playing or were you focused on the results of your actions? Were you in control of yourself before each pitch? Were you committed to your plan on each pitch? Asking yourself questions such as these and the others listed at the end of Chapter 5 helps you define failure in terms of things you can control.

Keep Your Mission in Mind

When you're struggling, the advice many people offer is "keep things in perspective." In our terms, they are telling you to get back in touch with your mission. Review your answers to the questions in Chapter 2, particularly to the question, "Why do you play baseball?"

It's a pretty safe bet that your answers did not include, "I enjoy mentally beating myself up after a loss," or "I love getting depressed after I make an error." The failure in baseball is part of what makes it a

> *"Baseball breaks your heart. It is designed to break your heart."*
> — *A. Bartlett Giamatti, former baseball commissioner*

great game, but the frustration, anger, pain and anxiety that come with it won't lead a list of reasons for why we play the game.

As discussed in Chapter 3, you choose the content of your thoughts. Focus on what you love about the game instead of negative events. Be aware of how much you enjoy the competition, the joking with your teammates, the smell of your leather glove or the feel of your cleats sinking into the grass. Enjoying the challenge rather than fighting it helps you leave a failure in the past and gets your mind where it needs to be to perform well — in the present.

Take the Bathtub Test

Put 2 inches of water in your bathtub and step into it with both feet. If you are able to stand on top of the water it's OK to demand perfection of yourself. If your feet come to rest on the bottom of the tub, however, what you've always known is obvious — you are not perfect.

Striving for perfection is admirable, but perfection as a measure of success is dangerous. Players often tie themselves into knots if they don't get a hit every time up or fail to hit their target with each pitch. Comparing yourself with the best player you've ever seen shows that errors, bad pitches and bad at bats happen to everyone. Giving yourself permission to make mistakes frees you from worrying about them. As we've said throughout the book, the more free you feel, the more likely you are to play your best.

Learn from It

Failure is feedback. It's like a yellow or red light indicating that you need to check in with yourself to determine how you can improve. It's saying you've now got an opportunity to learn.

Step back from your failure and examine it as someone else might see it. Pretend it happened to your best friend on the team. What would you say to

> *"What doesn't kill me makes me stronger."*
> — *Nietzsche*

him? Distancing yourself from the emotional impact of failing makes it much easier to draw the important lessens from it. Finally, force yourself to answer the question, "How can this experience help me become a better player?"

Succeeding as a "Role Player"

One of the main reasons you play baseball is to **play** baseball. You don't go through all the blood, sweat and tears of practice with the goal of sitting on the bench. Unfortunately, when you decide to play a team sport, control of playing time belongs to your coach. Lack of playing time is one of the most difficult challenges in baseball; it's the root of many mental game problems. Listed below are some suggestions for succeeding as a role player:

Ask Yourself, "Why Don't I Quit?"

What keeps you in baseball? These questions get right to the heart of the matter and are the key to making the most of your situation.

First, they help you recognize that staying on the team or leaving is your choice. Second, they put you back in touch with your motivation for playing. If you play because you love the game, go out and love practice and games. Playing and practicing with a sense of passion allows you to have a lot of fun and leads to your best performances. The better you play in practice and games the more playing time you are likely to get.

Also, operate from the perspective that it would be acceptable to stop playing. As distasteful as it may seem, leaving the team at an appropriate time is sometimes the best choice. As you consider this option, keep in mind the distinction between "quitting" and changing directions. If a pitcher throws three straight fastballs and they all are hit hard, is he quitting on his fastball if he then throws a curve? Of course not. Mixing in a breaking ball at this point would be a pretty good idea.

> Seriously considering leaving the team can be liberating. It can shift your focus from how you hate not playing to how you can get the most out of your experience. We aren't encouraging you to quit, but we do want you to choose an attitude and course of action that results in you getting the most enjoyment out of baseball.

One of the challenges of baseball is that the amount of playing time you get is outside of your control.

Focus on Your Circle of Control

Playing time is not within your circle of control. Regardless of how well you play, your coach makes the lineup. Since you can only control yourself, your challenge is to focus on being the best player you can be and trust that playing time will follow your improvement.

Developing your mental skills is still your responsibility. If you don't have many chances to play in games, you want to be at your best when you do get in. Skills such as your routines, breath and focal point will help you play consistently and improve your ability to be ready when you get called off the bench during a game.

The quality of your practice time is also important. If you are a hitter, make pregame batting practice your game. Make your time in the cage like an at bat during the game. Practice your routine, take your breaths and see how well you can trust yourself on each pitch just as you would in a game. Not only is this more fun than dragging yourself around frustrated with not starting, but the quality of your practice makes you a better player.

Build a support network of friends and family to help you deal with your disappointment over not playing. Make sure, however, that they support your efforts instead of talking negatively about the coach. Coach bashing might feel good at the moment, but it creates an angry and bitter attitude that hinders your performance. That attitude makes it much *less* likely that you'll see the playing time you're after. If your focus is "I'll never get a chance to play because coach hates me" instead of "How can I get better?," it's likely that you'll be correct.

Know Your Role

As much as it hurts to hear that you aren't a starter, most players like to know where they stand with the coach in relation to playing time. If your coach doesn't do a good job of clarifying your role on the team, ask him to do so. See how clearly you can define what you need to do to crack the starting lineup.

When the time comes to go into a game, be sure you're ready. According to United States Olympic pitching coach Jerry Weinstein, it's fine to be a cheerleader on the bench throughout much of the game, but a player must know when he needs to shift to focusing on the game from pitch to pitch. Even if your body isn't in the flow of the game, your mind can be connected with it. This enables you to be mentally prepared if your number is called.

Coming Back from Injury

Another difficult experience that can teach you a great deal is injury. Your first priority after an injury is to get quality treatment. Respect the trainer's and doctor's recommendations and give yourself the rest or treatment prescribed. Recovery can be as much mental as physical. The following ideas may be helpful as you start your journey.

Take Responsibility for Your Recovery

You are ultimately responsible for your own recovery, so take an active, intelligent approach to getting yourself back on the field. Your rehabilitation workouts now take the place of your games, so approach them that way. Mentally prepare yourself for them and focus on doing each exercise with as much quality as you can. Notice that we said "quality" not "mindless fury." Listen to your trainer and your body so you don't overdo it and re-injure yourself.

On the other hand, if your injury needs rest, make a point of getting quality rest. Stay off your leg if you're supposed to stay off it; don't throw if you're not supposed to throw.

Athletes often make the mistake of thinking that once their bodies are ready to play they can jump back into competition and be sharp, neglecting to regain their mental edge. There are a number of ideas you can use to stay mentally sharp when you are not physically able to play.

Imaging yourself facing batters, fielding ground balls and running the bases keeps your mind up to game speed. Mentally putting yourself in game situations, especially while watching a game, minimizes the time it takes you to readjust to the pace of the game. Similarly, if your injury allows it, "shadow" work (described in Chapter 9) is a great way to say sharp mentally and mechanically.

California Angels pitcher Mark Langston spent considerable time watching himself pitch on video while he was recovering from arm surgery. He felt that intently watching himself perform helped him stay in touch with his mechanics and his mental game, easing his transition back into pitching.

The relaxation procedures outlined in the Appendix will aid your imagery, control the stress of not playing and enhance your ability to control yourself once you do get back on the field. Relaxation has also been shown to physiologically aid the recovery process.

Injury is a learning opportunity. As you recover, focus on the progress you've made since the injury instead of how far you have to go to reach your pre-injury level.

Finally, maintain contact with your teammates when you are injured. It's easy to feel like an "outsider" when you aren't able to play, so make a point to avoid distancing yourself from the squad. They can be an important support group as you deal with not being able to play.

In short, take an active, intelligent approach to your recovery instead of becoming a passive victim sitting around feeling sorry for yourself.

Focus on Improvement

Focus on the progress you make since your injury instead of on how far you are from what you could do before the injury. Comparing your recovering performance to your pre-injury performance will result in frustration.

Face the Fear

Players commonly have to deal with some degree of fear when returning to competition after an injury. Questions such as "Will it hurt?" "Will I re-injure myself?" "Will I be able to play as well as I did before the injury?" and "Will I keep my starting spot?" can unnerve even the most confident players.

Much of this fear is helpful. You need to respect your injury and allow it to heal properly before returning to competition. A "healthy" fear of re-injuring yourself can help you do just that. On the other hand, fear that persists after you've been assured of full recovery is not helpful and distracts you from devoting your full focus to playing the game. Playing your best means throwing away any fears that aren't medically well-founded.

It can be difficult to determine if the fear is protective and should be respected (in which case consider not playing) or if you need to use your mental skills to let it go and focus fully on playing your best baseball. Discuss the matter directly with your trainer to make this decision.

Learn

Although you'd never ask to be injured, many players find that spending time on the injured list helps their careers. Use your extra time to develop mental skills and carefully observe the actions of your teammates and opponents. You gain important new perspectives on the game.

Life Outside of Baseball

Athletes often talk about how much the ideas in this book help them in their "performances" outside of baseball. Typical comments include: "I use the ideas when I'm taking an exam," and "It helps me stay in control during job interviews." In case you haven't picked up on it by now, this book is really about human performance, not just baseball. Whether you are taking an exam, asking a person out on a date, driving your car in a snowstorm or supervising a group of children, the ideas all apply.

Following are thoughts on how you can use the ideas in this book in the performance of your life.

Know Yourself

We have asked you a lot of questions in this book. If you've taken time to answer them you've learned much about yourself as a ballplayer. How well you know yourself both on and off the field is one of the most important issues in your life. You ultimately make every decision about what you do and how you perform, so the more you know about yourself the better your decisions will be!

You can learn a great deal about yourself playing baseball, but you can also gain important knowledge about yourself in any other arena. As you make your way through school, move in and out of relationships, work for employers, interact socially, manage your money, talk with your parents and generally move through life, pay attention to things like how you respond to stress, your strengths and weaknesses, who you most enjoy being with, what you enjoy doing, and what you need to do to be successful. Make each experience an opportunity to learn about yourself so you can become your own best coach. If you don't understand yourself, you can't expect others to understand you.

We started the book talking about how the goal of the mental game is to have confidence in your ability in baseball. Confidence is also a major goal in life outside of baseball. A strong sense of who you are can give you the confidence needed to take risks, explore new areas of life and have more fun.

If you might think you already know yourself or that knowing yourself sounds too "deep," keep your mind open and keep asking yourself the questions asked in this section. They take on more and different meanings as you mature.

Take Responsibility for Your Own Thinking

One of the main lessons you should have pulled from this book is the need to make intelligent choices about the content of your thoughts. This means taking an active approach to life and deciding what to think instead of allowing events around you dictate what goes on in your head. Remember, you can't control what happens you to, but you can control your response to it. Your attitude is a decision you make.

Attitude Is A Decision

One intelligent choice you can make is to focus on the aspects of each situation within your circle of control. Whether it's a tricky question on an exam, a traffic jam, a problem in a relationship or a concern over world hunger, your performance is best served by dedicating your efforts to the areas you have the ability to affect.

Taking responsibility for your thinking is difficult (_we_ certainly don't have it mastered). However, if you are mature enough to have continued reading this far, your thoughts are your responsibility. Actually, responsible thinking is really something you work _toward_ rather than something you achieve and simply "have," so make it part of your mission to strive to choose your own thoughts.

> _"A man is literally what he thinks, his character being the complete sum of all his thoughts."_
> **_— James Allen_**

Keep Your Mission in Mind

Jim Abbott wrote in his introduction that developing your mental game can help you gain "immense satisfaction with your career" knowing you gave the game all you had and made the most of your opportunity. Just as it's important to get clear on your mission in baseball, it's important to spend time thinking about what you want out of your life so it doesn't slip past you. What do you do that provides the greatest sense of satisfaction? What gives your life meaning? How would you like to be remembered after you're gone?

As we've emphasized, keeping answers to the "big picture" questions at the forefront of your mind can enhance your performance, provide you with a sense of direction and meaning, and minimize your stress. People often get so "caught up" in the effort to survive each day that they lose sight of the larger picture, fail to enjoy their present moments and end up regretting how they spent their time. Your mission also helps you overcome the adversity you face along your journey. In life, as in baseball, if you are not facing some adversity right now, it's on its way!

Respond to the questions in Chapter 2 from the perspective of your life outside baseball. Writing down your thoughts on the type of person you'd like to be and the feats you'd like to accomplish can help give you the "perspective" so important to living a fun and rewarding life. It can keep you from getting caught in the **go, go, go** mentality that results in your waking up one day wondering what the hell happened to your life.

> The challenge is then to put your life mission into action on a daily basis. If you want to be someone who is honest, hard working, and generous there is no reason to wait around. Figure out what you want to be like and be like that today. Likewise if you want to feel the immense satisfaction of significant accomplishments like graduating from college, buying your own car, getting a job in a field you love or establishing close personal relationships, you must take responsibility for making them happen.

Give Yourself a Present

Finally, our major theme has been to play baseball one pitch at a time. Off the field that translates into one "(<u>whatever you're doing</u>)" at a time. Just as playing one pitch at a time helps you play better and enjoy the game more, taking one "_____" at a time will enhance your performance and make it more fun.

The **self-control, plan, trust** model can be applied to getting a dance partner, taking an exam, discussing a problem with your friend or coach, managing your money, buying a car, negotiating a contract, dealing with the media, raising a child or any other "performance" you can think of.

You've got to be in control of yourself before you can control your performance, so start by checking in to see if you have a green light. If you don't, use your breath, a focal point, or a "release" to clear your thinking and get control. Next, clarify what you want to accomplish. Plan your life, plan your week, plan your day, plan your hour so you have a vivid picture in your mind of **what** you want to have happen and **how** you are going to accomplish it. Sometimes the only way to spend quality time with someone you care about, for example, is to commit to a time when you are going to break from your hectic schedules to get together.

Ultimately, the goal is to trust yourself and perform with a sense of personal freedom. Freedom means giving yourself permission to do what you want with your life and letting go of fear, stress, worry, doubt and concerns over what other people think. Trust usually isn't something you just "have" all the time. In fact, it's unlikely that anyone in his or her right mind lives free of fear all the time. Trusting yourself is fun and satisfying, however, so make a point to see how much time you can spend trusting yourself.

Developing your mental skills will not ensure success. Failure, disappointment and grief are parts of all our lives. You will have days when you don't have your "best stuff." Peak performance in life isn't about succeeding all the time or even being happy all the time. It's often about compensating, adjusting and doing the best you can with what you have right now.

Giving yourself the gift of the present helps keep you from getting so caught up in thinking the future will be better that you don't enjoy today. Throughout the book we have said right now is where the action and the enjoyment are — it's the only place you have control. We hope that this and the other ideas we have offered will help you find greater meaning and enjoyment in your life both in and out of baseball.

Appendix: Relaxation, Imagery and Self-Talk

Relaxation

Two of the main ideas of this book are the importance of being in control of yourself to control your performance, and practicing what you will be doing in a game. Relaxation training pulls these ideas together. Specifically, relaxation training provides an opportunity to practice controlling yourself in a comfortable environment allowing you to better control yourself in a game. In fact, you could say that relaxation training is to the mental game what the bullpen is to pitching and batting practice is to hitting.

Basic relaxation consists of lying on your back and relaxing yourself as deeply and fully as you can. Muscles should first be tensed and then released to experience the contrast between tension and relaxation. As you might expect, taking good deep breaths is also an important part of relaxation. The time needed for relaxation may range from five to 45 minutes, but normally 15-20 minutes are adequate. Specific methods will be provided shortly.

Relaxation benefits you in four ways:

1) **You learn to control yourself.** As discussed in Chapter 4, being in control of yourself requires the ability to recognize whether or not you are in control (check your traffic light) and then make needed adjustments. Because you focus so much on your body and your breathing, your awareness of what is going on inside you is increased (helping you see your internal traffic lights more clearly). Since the goal of relaxation is to let go of unwanted tension, it provides an opportunity to practice making that adjustment.

2) **Your ability to concentrate is enhanced.** During your relaxation periods there will be endless distractions caused by talking, phones ringing, cars driving by and your own thoughts, such as "I need to get that assignment done," "We need to win this game tonight," and "What should I get Mom for her birthday?" Overcoming these distractions by focusing on your body and breathing will develop your ability to concentrate. Learning to maintain your focus during relaxation will enhance your ability to focus during a game.

3) **The mind is quieted for enhanced imagery.** When you are relaxed, the "static" or "noise" in your mind caused by tension and random thoughts is minimized, allowing more vivid images. Just as a quiet environment while reading enhances your concentration abilities, you can image more clearly when you are relaxed. More about this will be covered shortly.

4) **Physiological benefits.** Regular relaxation practice has been shown to decrease heart and breathing rates, and blood pressure. Not only will it help your performance on the field, it can increase the quality of your life.

Some athletes think relaxation training sounds too "weird" or too far "out there" to try. That's understandable. There isn't anything very macho about it. Babe Ruth didn't do it, so why should you? Besides, many baseball people believe the way to get better is to get out on the field and bust your butt, not lay down and relax it! Hard work is mandatory for you to be successful, but if you can't control yourself during the game, the benefits of all that hard work will be "choked" off. Hopefully you will try it long enough to experience the many benefits it can give you, not the least of which is that it feels good!

How To Do Relaxation

The easiest way to do relaxation is to have somebody talk you through it. An outline for a relaxation script begins below for you or someone you know to record onto a cassette tape. Once the script is recorded, simply lie down and follow the instructions. If you would like to purchase a prerecorded relaxation and imagery tape, contact us at the address at the end of the Appendix.

In preparation for your relaxation session:

• Find a quiet, comfortable environment where you won't be disturbed for 10-20 minutes.

- If possible, lie down and place your arms by your side with your palms facing up. If you begin to feel discomfort in your lower back, bend your knees so that your feet are flat on the floor.
- Keep in mind that relaxation training isn't about lying perfectly still; if moving or scratching an itch makes you feel more comfortable, do it.

Doing relaxation during practice time not only gives players a chance to develop their mental skills, but also tells them that the coach thinks the mental game is important.

1) Begin by taking three deep breaths. Focus on the air as it enters and leaves your abdomen, letting the floor or chair support all of your weight.

2) Move through your body and follow the instructions provided here for each of the following body parts: right leg, left leg, buttocks, chest and abdomen, back, right arm and fist, left arm and fist, shoulders, and face.

Tense all of the muscles in each body part and hold it for approximately five seconds. Then release the tension and allow the body part to completely relax. Finally, take a deep breath, focusing on how warm and relaxed the body part is that you just tensed as you exhale. For example, say to yourself or on your tape: "Make a fist with your right hand and flex all of the muscles of your right arm... Tighten, tighten, hold it, hold it...... and relax. Let it go. Feel the warmth of that right arm as you take a deep breath in....... and out." (Repeat for each body part.)

3) After tensing and relaxing each body part, take a moment to scan your body for tension. Move your focus systematically from your toes up your legs, to your buttocks, back, abdomen, chest, up each arm from fingers to shoulders, and finally your face. If you find any tension, allow yourself to let it go.

4) Take time to enjoy the relaxed state you are in while maintaining your focus on your breathing and the feelings in your body.

Do some visualization when you are in a relaxed state. Outlines for imagery scripts for pitching, hitting and fielding that can be added to you relaxation procedure are in the next section.

When you are ready to come out of your relaxation, do it slowly by first wiggling your fingers and toes, fluttering your eyes open, and gradually working your way to a standing position.

Imagery

Often referred to as visualization, imagery is using your senses to create or recreate experiences in your mind. It can help your performance because the mind does not do a good job of distinguishing between what is real and what is imagined — the information is processed in similar ways. You have experienced this if you have ever had a dream where you woke up frightened or confused, had a fantasy that got you sexually aroused, or became scared when watching a good movie. These would never happen if your mind didn't interpret them as if they were real.

As mentioned throughout the book, visualization can be used at almost any time and place, and for any reason. You can do it in the shower, walking between classes, during batting practice or between pitches in a game. You can use it to mentally prepare for a game, to learn or practice a particular skill or mechanical change, to review your performance in a game, or to help speed your recovery from an injury. Seeing yourself playing well will build your confidence, while imagining yourself dealing with adversity will enhance your belief in your ability to handle any situation in which you find yourself. **There is a big difference between really doing imagery and just "thinking about the game." The greatest benefits come when you combine relaxation and imagery, and totally focus on your performance.**

Use visualization while watching yourself on video tape. Instead of passively watching the action, pretend you are out there; see how clearly you can see and feel what you were going through at the time.

See Me, Feel Me

The most effective imagery not only involves "seeing" pictures in your mind, but also your other senses. Ideally, in addition to picturing what you want to have happen, you also feel, hear and smell the action. Thus, the best imagery is like a total simulation of what you will or did actually experience while playing.

Many top performers in all fields are good at imagery and use it to gain valuable practice. In fact, since you can create any situation and have anything happen, a good imagery session is a great complement to your physical practice!

Checking Out Your Imagery Skills

As a warm-up, try this exercise: think for a few moments how you would tell someone to get from where you live to your home ballpark...

If you can think of how to get to the ballpark from your home, you can do imagery. You probably drew your directions from a picture of some sort in your head. It may have been a clear picture or it may have been more of a feeling. That's all imagery is. You do it every day. What we want you to do is learn to get better at it (be able to make the images clearer and have better control over them) and to do it with more purpose than you usually do.

"I just visualize who's on the mound and more or less have at bats over and over and over in my head and just sort of make it happen before it happens."
— Wade Boggs, New York Yankees

Now try recalling one of your greatest games. Put the book down and recreate scenes from the game as well as you can. See yourself performing; make the experience as real as possible.

What color uniforms are the teams wearing? What kind of a day is it? What sounds do you hear during and after your performance? What does it feel like when you are performing? What emotions do you experience afterward?

How vividly are you able to see, hear and feel that memory? Don't get upset if you couldn't see a thing. That's pretty normal. Some people never get clear pictures. Instead, they get much more into the feeling aspect of imagery. Others get clear pictures but not much feeling. Some image better with their eyes open, some with their eyes closed. Some players get images but can't control what they do with them. There are as many individual differences in imagery style as there are batting stances.

For one thing, keep in mind that, like other things in sports, the harder you try to image something, the harder it is to do. Relax and let the images come, don't force them.

The goal is to develop the ability to image clearly and have the ability to control your images. Any imagery skills you possess right now are useful to you the way they are, but they can become more helpful as you develop them through practice.

Internal and External Imagery

Go back to your memory of that great performance. Do you see yourself performing like you were watching yourself on TV or do you see what you actually saw while you were performing? Visualizing what *you* will see when you're performing is called "internal" imagery. Visualizing what others see when they watch you perform is called "external" imagery. Both views can be very helpful. External imagery is helpful when focusing on mechanics, but if you are able to do both, spend most of your time using internal imagery because you want the imagery to simulate what you will actually experience in a game.

Tips for Effective Visualization

- Work in as many senses as you can: see the action, feel yourself moving, hear the sounds, smell the smells.
- Make your images as vivid and clear as you can.
- Use internal imagery more than external imagery.
- See yourself doing things well.
- See yourself successfully overcoming mistakes, bad calls by the umpire or other forms of bad luck.

Imagery can be most effective when done during a relaxation session. Here are some ideas which can be read onto an audio cassette after the relaxation script presented earlier. Remember to involve as many senses as possible.

Pitching Imagery Ideas:

- Recall a time when you were pitching well. Mentally relive the thoughts, feelings and results you had during that inning or outing.

- Image yourself pitching well against the team you are about to face. See yourself successfully going through your pitching routine, retiring batter after batter.

- See yourself responding well to adversity. Visualize one of your fielders making an error, the umpire calling a pitch a ball that was clearly a strike or a batter hitting a double off the wall. See yourself keeping your composure, going through your strategy for releasing your frustration, anger or anxiety, and coming back to make good pitches to the next batter.

- If you are a starter, go through what you will experience over the entire day of your upcoming start. Include seeing yourself getting to the ballpark, getting changed, stretching out, throwing in the bullpen, throwing on the mound before the first inning, and facing the hitters in the first inning.

Hitting Imagery Ideas:

- Recall times when hitting seemed easy. See and feel yourself knock base hits all over the park. Remember how big the ball looked and hear the sound of the ball hitting the fat part of the bat. Feel the confidence you felt on those special times.

- See yourself having great at bats against your upcoming opponent. Image hitting against right- and left-handed pitchers. Remind yourself of what your plan is and see yourself executing it perfectly.

- Imagine being at the plate and swinging at a bad pitch or having the umpire call a strike on a ball you thought was low. See yourself step back, take a deep breath, perhaps go to your focal point to get yourself under control. Clarify your plan see yourself rope the next pitch up the middle for a base hit.

- Image yourself going through batting practice. Feel yourself being in a good mood — having fun and getting your work done. See yourself stepping into the cage with a clear purpose in mind and experience yourself hitting line drives to all parts of the field.

Fielding Imagery Ideas:

- Recall defensive plays that you have made in the past. Think of the best three plays you've ever made. Relive them in as much detail as you can.

- Image yourself cleanly making plays against your next opponent. Feel yourself go through your fielding actions with excellent mechanics.

- See yourself make an error. Go through your strategy to release that error — turn your back to the plate, take a deep breath, whatever you've decided to do — and then get ready for the next pitch. Hear yourself say, "Hit it to me." Finally, image yourself successfully make the next play.

Self-Talk

As you read this sentence, hear the words being pronounced in your head. Now hear them with an echo like the public address announcer at a stadium:

"Pinch hitting for Pedro Borbon...."

The running dialogue you have going on in your head (even when you aren't reading) is called your "self-talk." In fact, although you have thoughts you can't fully express verbally, you could say that thinking is talking to yourself. Thus, you do it all the time.

What do you say when you talk to yourself about your ability to play baseball? Remember that what you think often determines how you feel, and how you feel largely determines how you play. Your thinking consists of your self-talk, along with your imagery. Thus, the words you say to yourself impact how confident you feel, making self-talk a pretty important topic.

We aren't always aware of what we are saying to ourselves. That's a good thing because if we were aware of it all the time we'd go crazy (especially if it echoed like that public address announcer...). However, this is also dangerous because you may be talking trash to yourself without even knowing it. If you constantly bad-mouth yourself by saying "I stink," "I can't hit," or "I may never get anybody out again" but you aren't aware that you are doing it, you won't tell yourself to stop saying it!

Because of all the failure that is built into baseball, a lot of players spend a great deal of time talking negatively to themselves. Your self-talk is something you need to be aware of, at least to some degree. Most important though, make sure you choose to talk to yourself in an encouraging, confidence-enhancing way. In short, talk to yourself the way you'd talk to your best friend.

You can become more aware of your self-talk by getting into the habit of asking yourself, "What am I saying to myself about this?" and "Am I encouraging myself or discouraging myself?" Another way to stay in touch with what you are saying to yourself is to keep a journal. Each night or once a week write under the heading, "Here's What I Thought About My Baseball Playing Ability Today."

What should you say when you talk to yourself? Good self-talk statements are positive and encouraging ("I can rip this pitcher" or "I'm the man"). Secondly, say what you want to do ("I'm going to throw good low strikes"), not what you don't want to do ("I'm not going to walk anybody").

How to Use Self-Talk to Enhance Your Performance

Figuring out what you are saying to yourself when playing your best baseball will help you use self-talk to your best advantage. Say that to yourself whether you feel that way or not.

What are you saying to yourself when you are playing your best? Write it down here:

If you are like many players, your response was "Nothing, my mind is blank." OK, great, but **if you were** talking to yourself at those moments, what would you be saying? Having a phrase or a few phrases you know you say to yourself when you are playing well gives you something to go to when you are struggling.

Here are few examples of self-talk statements you can repeat to yourself anytime:

General:

- "I am in control of myself before each pitch."
- "I am taking one pitch at a time."
- "I am totally focused on each pitch."
- "I have paid the dues and I am trusting my ability."
- "Trust it."

Hitting:

- "I am a smart and strong hitter."
- "I am seeing the ball well and driving it hard."
- "Trust my hands."
- "See the ball."
- "Attack the ball."
- "Hit it hard."
- "Attack the top half of the ball."
- "Be aggressive."
- "Use the hands."
- "Put the fat part of the bat on the ball."
- "Use the whole field."

Pitching:

- "I'm in command of myself and my pitches."
- "Focus on the target, hit the target."
- "The ball is going right there."
- "Free and easy."
- "Stay back."
- "Let it go."
- "I'm the man."
- "Stay closed."

Fielding:

- "Hit it to me."
- "I can make any play."
- "I'm smooth."
- "Stay down."
- "Quick as a cat."

How Could It Help Me to Say Things I Don't Believe?

Sometimes, when you're feeling really low, saying confident statements to yourself like "I'm a great player" might sound laughable. There are a couple of reasons to do it anyway:

Tips For Effective Self-Talk

- Keep your self-talk as positive as possible.
- Keep your self-talk as task relevant as possible. Ask yourself "What do I need to do now?" instead of judging yourself or beating yourself up over an error or a loss.
- Make sure the last thought in your head before each pitch is positive and directs your focus to the task at hand.

---

1) It starts you in the right direction. The best players take responsibility for their own thinking: they choose what to think rather than letting the situation dictate to them what they should think.

2) Even if you don't "buy" what you are saying to yourself, making the effort to say positive things to yourself directs your focus and keeps you from saying anything negative. Your mind can't say, "I hope the ball gets hit to someone else," for example, when you have it saying, "Hit it to me." Thus, it gives you your best chance at being confident and performing great.

Finally, the chart below provides you with some examples of differences between ineffective and effective self-talk.

Ineffective (Not helpful)	**Effective (Helpful)**
• "Don't strike out here."	• "See the ball, hit the ball."
• "Don't hang this curve."	• "This one's going low and away."
• "I hope I don't make another error."	• "Hit it to me."
• "I stink."	• "Baseball is difficult. Things will go my way again if I focus on the process of playing the game."

To purchase an audio cassette of a relaxation and imagery session for baseball, write to:

Kinesis: Cassette Tapes
P.O. Box 7000-717
Redondo Beach, CA 90277

About the Authors

Ken Ravizza, Ph.D., is a professor of physical education at California State University-Fullerton and one of the top sport psychology consultants in the United States. Since entering the field 20 years ago, he has worked with the U.S. Olympic field hockey, water polo and equestrian

Ken Ravizza

teams, numerous individual Olympic and national-level competitors, the University of Nebraska football team and the NFL's New York Jets.

His baseball experience dates to 1980 when he became involved with the team at California State-Fullerton (which won the 1984 national championship) and since 1985 has worked in all levels of the California Angels organization as a sportpsych instructor. He is heavily involved with the Long Beach State team and has worked with many other collegiate programs, including UCLA and Arizona State.

He also has worked with international teams in India, Ireland, Sweden and Australia, and has been featured in numerous publications, including *The Sport Psychologist* and *Collegiate Baseball*.

Tom Hanson, Ph.D., is head baseball coach and assistant professor of physical education at Skidmore College in Saratoga Springs, N.Y. He earned his doctorate in sport psychology at the University of Virginia, and served as hitting coach for the school's baseball team.

Tom Hanson

He did his doctoral dissertation on the mental aspects of hitting, a project for which he interviewed notable players such as Rod Carew, Hank Aaron, Carl Yastrzemski, Tony Oliva, Stan Musial, Billy Williams and Pete Rose.

Hanson also coached at the University of Illinois while completing his master's degree. His undergraduate work was done at Luther College (Iowa) where he won all-conference honors and teams he played on won three conference championships.

He has worked with Ravizza in the Angels organization, was a writer in the book *Science of Coaching Baseball* (Jerry Kindall, editor) and has written several articles for sports publications. He is co-editor of the *Journal of Performance Education*, a publication of the University of Virginia's Center for Performance Education.

Notes

Quotes are from personal communications unless otherwise noted below.

Chapter 1

Winston Churchill; widely quoted.

Hank Aaron; from Hanson, T. (1992) *The Mental Aspects of Hitting: A Case Study of Hank Aaron.* Contemporary Thought on Performance Enhancement, 1, 49-70.

Chapter 2

Several ideas in this chapter are adaptations from Covey, S. (1989), *Seven Habits of Highly Effective People,* New York: Fireside.

Sisyphus story from Camus, A. (1955), *The Myth of Sisyphus and Other Essays,* New York: Vintage Books.

Ken Griffey Sr.; from Brandon, S. (1993), *Inside the Art of Hitting,* The Oregonian, July 15.

Bruce Barton; original reference unknown.

Dan Millman; from Millman, D. (1980), *Way of the Peaceful Warrior.* Tiburon, CA: H.J. Kramer, Inc.

Chapter 3

Greg Maddux; from Ballew, B. (1994), *Simply the Best,* Baseball America, July 11-24.

Circles of concern and control adapted from Covey, S. (see above).

Chapter 4

Orel Hershiser; from Hershiser, O. and Jenkins, J.B. (1989) *Out of the Blue,* Brentwood, TN: Wolgemuth & Hyatt.

Dennis Eckersley; from Etkin, Jack (1992), *Mind Game,* Bill Mazeroski's Baseball '92.

Mike Schmidt; Schmidt, M. & Ellis, R. (1994), *The Mike Schmidt Study.* Atlanta: McGriff & Bell, Inc.

Reasons to trust exercise adapted from Robbins, T. (1991), *Awaken the Giant Within.* New York: Summit Books.

Rick Dempsey; from Will, G. (1990), *Men at Work: The Craft of Baseball.* New York: Macmillan.

Chapter 5

Hank Aaron; from Hanson, T. (1992), (see above).

Aaron statistics; from Aaron, H., & Wheeler, L. (1991), *I Had a Hammer:The Hank Aaron Story.* New York: Harper Collins Publishers.

Al Kaline; from Falkner, D. (1990), *Nine Sides of the Diamond.* New York: Times Books.

Chapter 6

Orel Hershiser; from *Out of the Blue* (see above).

Chapter 7

Stan Musial; from Hanson, T. (1992), *The Mental Aspects of Hitting.* Unpublished doctoral dissertation, University of Virginia.

Tony Gwynn; from Stevenson, S. (1991), *Tony Gwynn: A Portrait of the Scientist in the Batter's Box.* New York Times, June 17.

Chapter 8

Ozzie Smith; Falkner, D. (1990), *Nine Sides of the Diamond.* New York: Times Books.

Dwight Evans; Falkner, D. (1990)

Chapter 9

Paul Molitor; from Etkin, J. (1992), (see above).

Chapter 10

A. Bartlett Giamatti; from Ferguson, H. (1991), *The Edge.* Cleveland: Getting The Edge Company.

James Allen; from Allen, J. (no year given), As a Man Thinketh. Marina Del Rey, CA: DeVross.

Appendix

Wade Boggs; from Etkin, J. (1992), (see above).